MUSKETS
TO MISSILES

Ontario Archives

Militiamen, Toronto, 1897

MUSKETS
TO MISSILES

A PICTORIAL HISTORY OF CANADA'S GROUND FORCES

By J.A. Foster

ⓝ METHUEN
Toronto New York London Sydney Auckland

Acknowlegement and thanks to Public Archives of
Canada, Royal Ontario Museum, Canadiana
Museum Branch of the Royal Ontario Museum,
Halifax Citadel Army Museum, Royal Canadian
Military Institute, National Gallery of Canada, Ontario
Archives, Public Archives of Nova Scotia, Military
Museum of Montreal, Archives Nationales du
Québec, Gravure Français au Canada, New York
Public Library and the research provided by Peter W.
Foster, without whose help this book could not have
been completed.

Canadian Cataloguing in Publication Data

Foster, Tony, 1932–
        Muskets to missiles

ISBN 0-458-81220-X

1. Canada – Militia – History – Pictorial works.
I. Title.

FC226.F68 1987   355.3'7'0971   C87-094255-7
F1028.F68 1987

Design: Robin Brass
Printed and bound in Canada
1 2 3 4   87   91 90 89 88

CONTENTS

Canadian troops digging reserve trenches in May 1918.

PAC PA3812

Soldier of Calgary Regiment on tank overlooking the
Italian city of Potenza, September 20, 1943.

Foreword

That many of the militia units in being today were formed before Confederation deserves special notice. That they have managed to survive the neglect, skilful or otherwise, of successive governments and lack of popular support for all these years is nothing short of miraculous. As a nation we should be ever grateful to the men who responded so readily in our times of need and to those who continue to man and maintain our militia units.

From the formation of the first units right through to the present day, it has been the same sad story of inadequate funding, equipment, accommodation and training; yet somehow these units managed to carry on through these periods of drought to provide the foundation on which were built the splendid armies of two world wars.

The Canadian Army that ended World War II in Europe was unique in many ways. Starting with a Regular Force of 4500 and a militia of 50,000, it had grown four years later to a force of some 600,000. These years of growth were not without their problems and we were fortunate to have been given the time necessary to ready the force for battle. The day had long gone when the militiaman could drop his plough, pick up his musket and take his place in the line. It required months to weed out the infirm and the incompetent and to train the new arrivals. The units that finally went to Italy and Western Europe bore little resemblance to those that had arrived in the UK some years earlier. When the time finally came, the men were probably the best trained of any in the Allied armies. What shortcomings have been commented on by the critics can nearly always be shown to have been the fault of the leaders from the top down; the men were splendid.

By the same token the units in action at the close of the war were greatly changed from those well trained but untried troops who first landed. Casualties and wastage had taken their toll and by the end they had become a sophisticated, battle-hardened force the like of which we had never seen before or since.

The business of war has become even more complex and complicated and it is now well nigh impossible for part-time militiamen, let alone regulars, to achieve the required standard. It took years last time and we have no assurance that we will be given the time again not only to train the officers and men, but of equal importance, to acquire the equipment.

Somehow or other "pax atomica" has kept us out of major conflict these many years—the longest period of peace in the century. Let us hope and pray that we may continue to avoid another war. In the meantime it is important to remember the past and draw strength and encouragement from the examples set by our forebears. It is important to give support to these present-day inheritors of our militia traditions and honour those who have gone before. It has been rightly said that "a nation that cannot remember its dead will soon cease to be worth dying for."

LIEUTENANT GENERAL ROBERT W. MONCEL, OBE, DSO.

"A View of the Taking of Quebec September 13th, 1759. Showing the manner of debarking the English Forces, and of the resolute scrambling of the light Infantry, up a Woody Precipice to dislodge the Captains post, which defended a small entrenched path, through which the Troops were to pass. Also a view of the signal Victory obtained over the French regulars, Canadians and Indians which produced the surrender of Quebec."

Royal Ontario Museum, Toronto

Canon Sur son affeu de la plus haute.
uolée et du plus gros calibre

CONTEST FOR A CONTINENT

The Beginnings

For a European of 1627 the distant New World was a place of uncertainty and mystery—at least to those who knew anything about it at all. The Dutch, Spaniards, French, Portuguese and English were laying claim to various portions of the two western continents. They came seeking opportunities to do God's work or to find gold, trade or women, although not necessarily in that order. Over the next two hundred years nearly every European war had its parallel conflict in the New World.

An inept 27-year-old Charles I sat on the British throne. The dour young Oliver Cromwell had already decided to contest the Huntingdon seat for Parliament the following year. After a faltering start, the founding of Jamestown, Virginia, in 1607 and the landing of the *Mayflower* at Massachusetts Bay in 1620 had opened the way for development of England's first North American colonies.

Across the English Channel, Louis XIII ruled France on the advice and under the influence of Cardinal Richelieu, the Church's master political intriguer. As far back as 1535, French explorers like Jacques Cartier had pushed far up the St. Lawrence River. Those that followed were now fanning out in a sweep from Acadie (later to become Nova Scotia) to beyond the Great Lakes. In their search for skins and furs these trappers, soldiers and Catholic missionaries of New France moved deep into the forest wilderness, first fighting then trying to convert the indigenous Indian population.

By 1608, Quebec (*Kebec* , "the narrowing place" in the Huron language) an Indian settlement at the first narrows of the St. Lawrence River, had become France's capital of the New World. Realizing that

Quebec provided the key that would unlock the doors to all the waterways on the North American continent, Samuel de Champlain chose the site to build his first *habitation*. It consisted of three two-storey wood buildings surrounded by a palisade at the foot of what is today Mountain Street. Of the 32 founding colonists, he arrested four and hanged one for plotting to murder him. Twenty-seven years later when he died there were still fewer than 300 whites in the whole of Canada while over the same period the population of the English colonies along the Atlantic seaboard had increased from zero to 7000; this ratio remained fairly consistent throughout the entire French occupation of Canada.

The greatest threat to the colony's existence throughout the early years remained the Indian Iroquois Confederacy. The Iroquois, allies first of the Dutch then later, after the fall of New Amsterdam (New York) in 1664, of the British, remained a scourge to the French for nearly a century. To combat them the colonists used swords and muskets brought with them from the Old World and protected their primitive fortifications at Port Royal and Quebec with small cannon.

The earliest recorded evidence of an organized defence force dates from 1627 when all male settlers agreed voluntarily to defend themselves collectively against the Indians. Eight years later, Chevalier de Montmagny, the military governor, made it official by enrolling male colonists in a proper militia force and providing them with military training. The colony's government operated under a confusing troika; the governor commanded the army, the intendant controlled the finances and the bishop ruled the Church and the administration of justice. The continuous quarrelling that resulted from this odd arrangement lasted until the British capture of Quebec nearly 150 years later.

To protect the new religious post of Ville Marie (later Montreal) 150 miles upriver from Quebec, Montmagny organized 50-man flying squads. At first the Indians' hit-and-run fighting tactics baffled the French settlers, but they learned quickly how to defend against sneak attacks and, when going on the offensive, to use the natural forest cover to their advantage. Often the hardy backwoodsmen dressed like the Indians, resplendent with war paint and feathers. In spite of the harsh climate, starvation, threat of massacre and lack of supplies from France, the fragile settlements in Acadie and along the St. Lawrence River survived and grew.

Meanwhile, in the Old World, English Puritan forces led by Cromwell defeated the armies of Charles I at the battles of Marston Moor and Naseby. The king surrendered, was brought to trial and sentenced to death. He died with great dignity on the chopping block before Whitehall Palace on January 30, 1649. Eleven years later Cromwell too was dead. Charles II ascended the English throne.

In 1643 the five-year-old Dauphin became Louis XIV of France and began a spectacular 72-year reign, the longest rule of any monarch before or since. Initially Regency power rested with his mother, Anne of Austria, and her minister, until his death in 1661, when Louis began his era of personal government. Under his able generals Turenne and Condé the French army became the finest fighting machine in Europe.

To combat the growing slaughter of colonists by the Indians, Louis sent "one good regiment of infantry" to New France in 1665. The population had grown to 550 souls, of which one quarter were priests and nuns. The well trained and equipped French regulars looked upon the native Canadian militiamen as barbarians; but that opinion changed swiftly after a few sharp encounters with the Iroquois. Accustomed to standing and fighting pitched battles in the open, the disciplined French regulars died bravely but somewhat pointlessly. A few "barbarian" militiamen were encouraged to join the depleted ranks of regulars and in a short time taught the uniformed novices the art of staying alive and out of sight in hostile Indian country.

To provide for a continuous population growth Louis instituted *les filles du roi,* "the King's Daughters," as breeding stock. Shipped overseas in batches of 150, these country girls from the west of France were selected for their wide hips and strong legs and backs. All were certified by their local priests as spinsters before embarkation. Baron de Lahontan described one arrival at Quebec.

"Several ships were sent hither from France with a Cargo of Women of an ordinary reputation under the direction of some old stale Nuns who ranged them in three classes. The Vestal Virgins were heap'd up (if I may so speak) one above another in three different apartments, where the bridegrooms singled out their brides, just as a butcher does a ewe from amongst a flock of sheep... the fattest went off best, upon the apprehension that these, being less active, would keep truer to their engagements and hold out better against the nipping cold of winter...."

With the threat of Indian massacre reduced, Louis recalled 20 of the 24 companies to fight in his European wars, in which he made himself master of the Netherlands and Burgundy. To compensate the colony for its loss of troops he ordered the new governor, Comte de Frontenac, to organize a permanent militia. All males between the ages of 16 and 60 were liable for service. Although the governor provided arms for each man, there were no uniforms or pay. The militiamen were placed under command of the regular troops, who used them for moving supplies and building bridges in addition to normal military duties. To protect his far ranging voyageur trappers from the avenging Iroquois, Frontenac built a series of small forts along the Great Lakes route. One, where the St. Lawrence flows out of Lake Ontario he named after himself; it later became the city of Kingston.

Hostility between France and England in the New World deepened as England began expanding her own formidable fur-trading empire into the rich hunting grounds around Hudson Bay. Concerned about France's power, the English colonies in the south began arming their Indians. Raiding parties were encouraged to attack any French settlement. Fifteen hundred Iroquois massacred the inhabitants of Lachine then threatened Montreal. A hundred and twenty prisoners were captured and led away to the torture stakes. Alarmed, Louis sent the still-fierce 70-

year-old Frontenac back from France to rally the colonists.

The imperious old firebrand decided to take the initiative and attack the English outposts. Made up of a combination of militiamen, wild hard-drinking Métis and unmanageable Christian Indians, his three striking forces snowshoed south to invade Maine, New Hampshire and New York. They scored a succession of brutal victories before withdrawing. The village of Schenectady was burned to the ground while 38 men, 10 women and 12 children were butchered with tomahawks and scalping knives.

Frontenac wrote: "You cannot believe the joy that this slight success has caused, and how much it contributes to raise the people from their dejection and terror." The French discovered to their astonishment that they were just as capable of fighting the British on their home ground as fighting the Indians. For the first time the disunited English colonists realized that they must either destroy Canada or be destroyed. A series of wars followed that was to last for the next 70 years.

A retaliatory British force of 34 ships and 2000 men commanded by Sir William Phips dropped anchor in front of Quebec in mid-October 1690. A junior officer went ashore under a flag of truce. He was brought blindfolded before Frontenac and the powerful men who ruled Canada. "The men were dressed so splendidly that it made small difference taking the cloth from my eyes. I was dazzled by looking at them," he reported. The old governor flung the surrender demand on the floor. "I will answer your general only from the mouths of my cannon."

Three days later, after failing to break the line held by Frontenac's men on the Beauport shore and receiving a taste of the French cannons, Phips withdrew downriver. Once more Canadian spirits soared and for nearly two decades a period of relative stability settled over the New World. The Canadians pushed westwards to the Great Lakes and beyond. They founded Detroit in 1701. Yet despite these far ranging explorations the French remained thinly spread and no match for the growing population of the 12 (later, Georgia became the 13th) English-speaking colonies, which by 1705 had passed 200,000.

In Europe, upon the death of Charles II of Spain, the Spanish crown passed to Louis' second grand-

Royal Ontario Museum, Toronto

A European powder horn, 18th century, made of trimmed cattle horn bound with hammered brass.

son, Philip, precipitating the War of the Spanish Succession between France and Spain and a coalition of European states led by England, Austria and the Netherlands. By the time it ended a decade later Spain and France were in economic ruins and reduced to second class powers, mainly as the result of the Duke of Marlborough's brilliant Continental victories.

The Treaty of Utrecht in 1713 gave Britain Gibraltar, the islands of Minorca and Newfoundland, Nova Scotia (which included the area that was to become New Brunswick) and a clear field in Rupert's Land, (now the northern portions of Quebec, Ontario, Manitoba and Saskatchewan and a part of Alberta and the Northwest Territories). Although peace had officially returned to Europe and the New World, the French and English colonies continued building their defenses for the war they were certain would one day come to settle final ownership of the North American continent.

(Overleaf)
"A View of the Landing of the New England Forces in the Expedition against Cape Breton, 1745." The landing parties head ashore after the siege of 40 days to attack the fortress of Louisbourg in the rear.

Royal Ontario Museum, Toronto

Halifax Citadel Collection

Maj.-Gen Jeffrey Amherst (1717-1797) commanded the army that captured Louisbourg in 1758. He was made commander in chief of forces in North America and was the architect of the campaign against the French that culminated in the fall of Quebec in 1759 and the capture of Montreal in 1760.

The Struggle for Dominance

As a defence and protection of their supply lines into the Gulf of St. Lawrence, the French began building Fortress Louisbourg on Cape Breton Island. With 219 cannon and 17 mortar, it was "a stupendous fortress" according to French-Canadian historian the Abbé Casgrain. It came to be recognized as the strongest fortress in North America at the time. Complaints about this French threat to the economic well-being of the English colonies came loud and clear to Governor Shirley of Massachusetts. In the early summer of 1745 he organized a British naval squadron under Admiral Warren with a landing force commanded by Gen. Pepperell to capture Louisbourg. Pepperell's crafty Yankee regulars and militia attacked its poorly defended rear. After a five-week siege Governor Duchambon surrendered.

This spectacular victory turned out to be short-lived. Under the Treaty of Aix-la-Chapelle in 1748, ending the war of the Austrian Succession, England restored Louisbourg to the French. The nearly apoplectic Governor Shirley sent a bitterly worded letter to London. Hoping to restore some balance of power to the area, the government sent Charles Cornwallis with a fleet of ships and settlers in 1749 to build a fortress settlement of its own on the site of what is now the city of Halifax. Invested as governor of Nova Scotia, Cornwallis authorized the raising of a provincial militia.

Battle lines were drawn. The population of the 13 English colonies numbered 1,500,000, including 200,000 white men of military age. Canadians in the same age group numbered fewer than 20,000. Yet the Indian chiefs, knowing the steely determination and adaptability to hardship of the Canadians, were certain that they would emerge the victors.

Neither British nor French army commanders sent out to the colonies understood what they were facing. In a hundred years the military defence experts in Paris and London had learned nothing. Resolutely they clung to their conviction that battles in the wilds and backwoods of North America could be fought along conventional European lines.

Hostilities opened in 1753-54 with a number of fierce skirmishes over trading rights in the Ohio River valley, then spread to Pennsylvania, New York and the other border states. Near Fort Duquesne (Pittsburgh today) the 21- year-old Maj. George Washington opened fire on a Canadian patrol, killing ten men, including its commander Coulon de Jumonville. Later, after a counterattack, Washington was captured but allowed to return home with his surviving men after signing a surrender document. Washington, who knew no French, thought that by admitting to "l'assassinat du Sieur de Jumonville" he was agreeing that Jumonville had died in battle. The signed document would return to haunt him throughout his career.

The following year Maj.-Gen. Edward Braddock marched 2000 superbly trained redcoats and the best of the Virginian bluecoated militia into the northern woods. As the army moved, 300 burly axemen led the way, hacking out a 12-foot pathway for the wagons, cattle and guns. The entourage reached a ford on the Monongahela River and began crossing in tightly disciplined marching order; the short red-faced Braddock was a stickler for appearances.

A force of 600 Indians, 150 Canadian militia and 85 French regulars waited silently in the woods ahead. When the brilliant red and white targets came within range they opened fire. Men and horses fell in heaps. The fearless Braddock refused to withdraw into the forest. For two hours he raged, cursing and beating his men with the flat of his sword if they tried making for cover. Four horses were shot out from under him. Finally, a musket ball brought him crashing to the ground. "We shall better know how to deal with them another time," he murmured as he died. His adjutant, George Washington, whose clothes were riddled with bullet holes, led the shamefaced remnants of the army home.

Placing boneheaded military commanders in the field was not exclusively a prerogative of the English. In late August 1755, German Baron Dieskau led 3000 whitecoated French regulars to defeat against a mix of 300 Iroquois and assorted American militia at Lake George, New York. His army was routed and the surprised Dieskau wounded and captured. In New York on his way home to Europe he complemented his foes. "Ach, the American militia fight like good boys in the morning, like men at noon and like devils in the afternoon."

Although the lands of Acadie were now under nominal English rule the French maintained Fort Beauséjour at the narrows onto the Acadian peninsula on the borders of what are now New Brunswick

Louis-Joseph, Marquis de Montcalm (1712-1759), entered the army at the age of nine. He was made commander in chief of French forces in North America in 1756 but was under the authority of the governor general of New France, Vaudreuil, with whom he feuded. Montcalm favoured the traditional European approach to warfare, while Vaudreuil favoured the flexible guerilla tactics he had learned on the North American frontier.

(Overleaf)
"A View of Louisburg in North America, taken near the Light House when that City was besieged in 1758."

and Nova Scotia. Beauséjour had changed hands several times over the century since Champlain founded it. By 1755 most of the 9000 Acadians in the region had taken a conditional oath of allegiance to the English king and asked for nothing more than to be left in peace to attend to their farms. But their priests would have none of it; the oath of allegiance meant nothing, they said. One fanatical priest, Abbé Joseph Louis Le Loutre, promised his flock death at the stake and perdition if they deserted France.

The Abbé offered 100 livres for every English scalp, personally supervising how the knife should cut across the victim's head. In a two-year period he recorded payments for 110 of these grisly specimens. Fed up with his antics, the English attacked him at Beaubassin, whereupon he burned the village and led his parishioners to the safety of Fort Beauséjour, where he remained a thorn in the British hide and an embarrassment to the fort's weak-hearted governor, Captain Vergor. To settle the matter once and for all, 2000 New England militiamen backed by a few British regulars and led by 28-year-old Brigadier Robert Monckton were landed from the sea unopposed and started a bombardment in preparation for their attack.

One of the first shells exploded inside a bomb shelter where six French officers were at their *petit déjeuner*. All were killed. Vergor and the Abbé, sitting in an adjacent shelter, were so terrified that they surrendered the fort. The Abbé escaped, disguised as a farmer, while Vergor invited Monckton to supper to celebrate his victory. The victor accepted contemptuously. There was a splendid irony to the occasion: Vergor's father had been the governor of Louisbourg and surrendered it in 1745.

In Halifax, Governor Charles Lawrence ordered an Acadian delegation to Government House to take a new and unconditional oath of allegiance to the Crown. They refused. Lawrence eyed them coldly. "Then you are no longer subjects of the King of England but of the King of France. You will be treated as such and removed from the country."

Thus began the Acadian Expulsion in which 6000 people were uprooted and carried away for distribution among the English colonies along the Atlantic coast. New England Colonel John Winslow wrote to the barely literate Monckton, who commanded the expulsion, that the affair "looks odd, and will appear so in future history."

Meanwhile, the French Indian allies were rampaging in an orgy of pillage, rape and butchery along the Ohio Valley. One indignant settler wrote to the governor of Pennsylvania: "It is really very shocking for the husband to see the wife of his bosom, her head cut off and the children's blood drunk like water by these bloody cruel savages."

In the summer of 1756, the commandant of Fort Duquesne, Capt. Jean Daniel Dumas, received so many scalps that it took eight days to hand out payments to the various Indian scalping parties. He wrote to his superiors: "I have succeeded in ruining three adjacent provinces, Pennsylvania, Maryland and Virginia, driving off the inhabitants and totally destroying the settlements over a tract of country thirty leagues wide.... I had six or seven different war parties in the field at once, always accompanied by Frenchmen." War parties came to within 50 miles of Philadelphia, then the largest English-speaking city in the world after London. They burned farms 60 miles from Boston. Citizens of Maryland were offered £50 for the scalp of every enemy Indian over the age of 10. Most frontier families either fled or died.

In the spring of 1755 hostilities between France and England were renewed officially by the Seven Years War in Europe. A series of strategically brilliant campaigns was fought by Frederick the Great of Prussia, aided with subsidies and troops from England, against a coalition of Austria, Russia, France, Sweden and Saxony. In North American the French were triumphant in the west, beaten back in Acadie and contained in the area of Lake George in upper New York State.

France sent the gallant Marquis de Montcalm to command its North American forces while England dispatched the incompetent Earl of Loudon and Gen. Abercrombie to command theirs. Montcalm had no sooner arrived in Quebec than he opened operations by capturing and destroying Fort Oswego, an English post on Lake Ontario that the British intended using as a base for a projected attack against the French fort at Niagara. From Oswego Montcalm hurried northeast to Lake Champlain and entrenched himself at Fort Ticonderoga. For the moment he had secured the west and barred the entrance gate into Lower Canada.

Lord Loudon meantime talked a great deal but did

"A View of the Landing Place above the Town of Quebec, describing the Assault of the Enemys Post, on the Banks of the River St. Lawrence, with a Distant View of the Action between the British and French Armys, on the hauteurs D'Abraham…"

nothing. The following year he started for Halifax on his way to attack Louisbourg. But unlike the decisive Pepperell a decade earlier, he wasted months of precious time in spectacular preparations for his assault. With Loudon safely out of the way and busy playing his war games, Montcalm sailed promptly from Fort Ticonderoga and laid siege to Fort William Henry with 6000 men. The garrison surrendered after being given a pledge of safety against the Indians and the right to march unarmed to nearby Fort Edward, whose cowardly garrison commander and 3600 men had refused to assist the beleaguered defenders.

Unfortunately Montcalm could not bind his savage allies to a Frenchman's word of honour. As the defeated British and their families marched out of Fort William Henry, the forest glades erupted suddenly with Indian war-whoops. Short of ordering his troops to shoot down the Indians, Montcalm and his

The death of the Marquis de Montcalm. This is a stylized
painting of the event. Montcalm, mortally wounded, died
in Quebec the day after the battle.

officers did everything they could to prevent the
slaughter. His failure to defend these helpless men,
women and children with his full force remains a stain
on an otherwise noble character and career.

Yet despite French triumphs in the struggle for
America the end was at hand. In England William Pitt
took over the reins of government. Like every great
ruler and statesman Pitt recognized that the success
of a war, campaign or battle depends not so much
upon the soldiers who are led as on the soldiers who
lead. Pitt decided correctly that as long as the
continent's two principal bastions remained in French
hands there could be no peace. To solve the problem
once and for all in 1758 he sent Gen. Sir Jeffrey
Amherst (later Field Marshal Lord Amherst), Maj.-
Gen. James Wolfe and Admiral Boscawen with an
army and a fleet of ships to reduce Louisbourg and
capture Quebec.

In the same year the government in Quebec passed the Militia Act requiring compulsory militia service for all able-bodied men. The regulations called for "muster parades every 6 months, drills every 3 months. Each man to provide a musket, gun or fusil not less than 3 feet long in barrel, two extra flints and 12 charges of powder and ball." Secure in their seemingly impregnable fortresses, the French waited for the British to appear.

Four thousand citizens lived behind the mighty ramparts of Louisbourg, guarded by 3800 regular troops and 3000 sailors. Every male inhabitant—storekeeper, smuggler and drunk—was pressed into temporary militia service. When the sails of Boscawen's 39 ships were sighted through the rainswept Cape Breton mists, Governor Chevalier de Duchambon's forces stood ready in the fortress and on the beaches to repel the invaders.

For over a week gale winds, snow-squalls and howling rainstorms kept Amherst and his 12,000 soldiers on board the ships. Finally, on the morning of June 8 the normally cautious Amherst ordered the attack to go in. Wolfe, whose division made the main assault at Freshwater Cove, described the landings as "rash and ill-advised." Fifty-two days later Duchambon raised the white flag. With the surrender all Cape Breton and Prince Edward Island went to the British, while the great fortress itself, after months of destructive labour, was levelled to the ground. With summer almost over Amherst decided to postpone his attack on Quebec until the following year.

Meanwhile, in the west, Gen. Abercrombie, without waiting for his cannon to get into position, hurled 15,000 men against Montcalm at Ticonderoga.

Lord Howe, who had been sent to do Abercrombie's thinking for him, had died earlier on the trail from a musket volley. Wolfe called him "the noblest English-man that has appeared in my time and the best soldier in the British Army." Howe had realized the need to adapt his forces to the realities of wilderness fighting; troops were ordered to discard their powdered wigs, cut their hair, paint their musket barrels to prevent glitter, and cut the tails from their red uniform jackets to make travel through the bush easier.

Abercrombie was no Howe. The fortress of logs and palings remained invulnerable to the claymores of the Highlanders and repeated English charges. Abercrombie panicked and without firing a single cannon shot against the 3100 men inside Ticonderoga withdrew to Fort William Henry, leaving 2000 dead. Montcalm exaggerated ecstatically. "Without Indians, almost without Canadians or colony troops... I have beaten an army of 25,000." It was to be the last important French triumph on the continent.

Gen. Bradstreet, with a force of colonial militia, crossed Lake Ontario and captured Fort Frontenac with its rich stores and several French lake vessels. A few months later Gen. Forbes forced the capitulation of Fort Duquesne and in its place erected Fort Pitt, in later years the city of Pittsburgh. By spring of 1759 the English were mounting three armed expeditions to administer the coup de grace.

The first captured Fort Niagara and defeated the French relieving force. Gen. Amherst's group marched on Lake George, forcing the French to blow up Ticonderoga and retreat to Crown Point, from where their ships still maintained supremacy on Lake Champlain. Amherst spent the rest of the summer

Sword used by the Marquis de Montcalm at the Battle of Quebec.

building vessels to meet the challenge. The third force of 9000 carefully selected troops under Gen. Wolfe sailed up the St. Lawrence to Quebec. Behind the citadel's frowning ramparts that bristled over the great cliffs, Montcalm waited with 15,000 regulars and 1000 Indians.

Wolfe planned to tempt his opponent out to battle. He divided his forces and built a variety of redoubts from where he could harass the defenders with shot and shell, gradually battering down the city's walls. Montcalm refused to take the bait although Wolfe's gunners seriously weakened his outer defence perimeter. The summer passed. Wolfe tried a desperate attack upon the Beauport trench lines, behind which lay Montcalm's serried masses of troops. It failed. After losing 500 men Wolfe withdrew. Inside the impregnable fortress Quebec spirits soared.

Autumn came. Food grew scarce. Wolfe fell ill. The troops started to grumble about the hopelessness of their situation. Wolfe decided on one last desperate attempt to advance up to the heights of the Plains of Abraham before abandoning the expedition to the approach of winter. Discovery of the secret night time movement would mean annihilation for the British forces; success would mean facing an army twice its size and in the best of health and spirits. Yet the plan succeeded and as dawn broke on the morning of September 13, 1759, British troops stood on the Plains and faced the last great army of France in North America.

Wolfe ordered his troops to hold their fire until the enemy was within 40 yards. At 10 in the morning, to the sound of the *pas de charge* drumbeat Montcalm's Canadians moved forward. At 130 yards the line halted to fire. The gaps in the British line closed up. Two English cannon erupted suddenly, plowing a path of destruction and blood through the advancing barefoot and moccasin-clad Canadians mixed in with the French regulars in their buckled shoes and gaiters. The line wavered, then pressed forward again to fire. More gaps in the British line. "Close up your lines! Hold your fire!" the British sergeants roared. At 40 yards Wolfe ordered: "Give fire!" The British drummers tapped the order out across the field. Two iron balls exploded from every Brown Bess on the British front line.

The troops advanced in a smooth practised rhythm—reload powder and ball—ram home—march forward 10 paces to clear the musket smoke—aim—fire. The French line broke at 10:15 a.m. Wolfe, already twice wounded, fell with a musket ball through his chest. He died on the battlefield with the cheers of his victorious troops ringing in his ears. In the rout that followed Montcalm was also mortally wounded. He rode back into the city and died the following day. On September 17, the Lilies of France were hauled down from the flagstaff atop the great ramparts and the British Standard hoisted in their place.

De Lévis succeeded Montcalm and withdrew his forces to Montreal. A year later he found himself hemmed in by 17,000 British troops and was forced to capitulate. De Vaudreuil, the last governor-general of New France, surrendered the whole country. The 60,000 Frenchmen in the New World had put up a brilliant and gallant fight against the continent's million and a quarter Englishmen. History might fault the French governors, intendants and administrators for corruption, venality and greed but never courage and devotion to duty by the soldiers, militia and citizenry of New France.

The Treaty of Paris signed in 1763 officially closed two centuries of struggle. France surrendered everything in America except Louisiana, the islands of St. Pierre and Miquelon and certain fishing privileges in Newfoundland. Spain gave up Florida, and England became mistress of the western world in North America at the same moment she became the dominant power in India and the Far East.

(Facing page)
The death of General Wolfe at Quebec.

Royal Ontario Museum, Toronto

The hilt of the sword used by Gen. Richard Montgomery, one of the commanders of the American forces that attacked Quebec City on New Year's Eve, 1775.

RIVALRY AND REVOLUTION

Ironically, victory over the French in Quebec contributed indirectly to England's loss of her 13 American colonies. The victory bonfires of rejoicing that lit the coastal New England villages and the marketplaces in New York and Philadelphia were the last of their kind in American history. Between 1759 and 1764 Canada remained under British martial law. The French militia system for colonial defence was maintained and as a result the Indian attacks organized by Chief Pontiac were successfully dealt with by Canadian—and later American—militia units. The British generals were most impressed.

The political leadership of the colonies had developed grievances against the mother country. If London had shown any understanding towards them or if they had felt any loyalty towards the Crown, the Revolution could have been avoided. However, with few exceptions, America's leaders were not monarchists by conviction. The upper classes, on the other hand, were and remained loyal to the end, eventually becoming the bone and sinew of the growing English-speaking populations of Canada and Acadie.

The great mass of colonists were republicans by nature, contemptuous of overseas institutions and authority; many were emigrants, such as the Quakers of Pennsylvania and the Puritans of New England, who had left England because of suffering and discontent to find a better freer life. It required only the self-confidence of pioneer life and the friction of a few unpleasant controversies to provide the tinder that kindled the flame of rebellion. Yet with all their grievances—the Stamp Act, taxation without representation, the arrogance of British officers and the incapacity of British generals and statesmen—it was not until 1775 that a clear majority of the populace was in favour of actual war. A strong minority was violently opposed to it. Even after the Declaration of Independence skilled statecraft and good generalship by the British might have turned the rebels into a small minority. But it was the rebels, not the British, who had the statesmen and speakers—giant men like George Washington and the firebrand orator and hypocrite Patrick Henry, a Southern slave owner who cried: "Give me liberty or give me death!"

The Quebec Act of 1774 formulated by Wolfe's cold grey-eyed quartermaster-general, Guy Carleton, extended the limits of the Province of Quebec (New France became officially the Province of Quebec in 1763) to cover the French settlers along the shores of the Great Lakes, south into the Ohio Valley and north and west to the Mississippi, Red River and Lake Winnipeg. It granted also large territories to the Indians. The act provided for freedom of worship for French-Canadian Catholics. The English colonies were aghast; the extremist Protestant New Englanders were up in arms. The September 1774 Congress at Philadelphia approved an "Address to the people of England" which, after referring to the arbitrary English rule under which the French-Canadians were said to suffer—near total freedom when compared to the liberty previously accorded them by France, stated: "Nor can we suppress our astonishment that a British Parliament should ever consent to establish in that country a religion that has deluged your island with blood and dispersed impiety, persecution, murder and rebellion through every part of the world."

An American call to arms the following year found the French of both Acadie and Quebec indifferent to the purple prose emanating from Philadelphia. Even Washington's special appeal—translated into French

Gen. Richard Montgomery's beautifully carved powder horn.

—urging insurrection created little more than passing interest. Fortunately the government of Quebec was in Carleton's capable hands. The fact that Canada today is a nation independent from the United States can be traced directly to his foresight and courage. Had he, and not Sir William Howe, been placed in command and given a free hand in the English colonies he could have suppressed the rebellion and captured Washington in the winter of his discontent and wretchedness at Valley Forge. But destiny had decided on an alternate solution.

Carleton had only a few hundred regulars under his command when the riots in the 13 colonies had developed into a revolution. After the battles at Lexington in April 1775 and Bunker Hill two months later and Ethan Ellan's capture of the forts of Ticonderoga and Crown Point, the historic warpath into the Province of Quebec lay open. Congress created a Continental Army under George Washington. Two American armies led by Benedict Arnold and Richard Montgomery marched north to capture Montreal and besiege the city of Quebec. Montgomery had fought with Wolfe and Amherst and knew Carleton well. Disguised as a fisherman, Carleton slipped out of Montreal and went on to defeat and kill Montgomery

then rout Arnold on Lake Champlain. Although the Canadian territories remained secure, the revolutionary upheaval within the 13 colonies continued. American success was assured finally with the signing of the Franco-American Alliance in 1778 (joined by Spain the following year).

For six years competent and incompetent generals played and plundered, seized and wasted opportunities until the prestige of revolution had faded and the mass of people were heartily sick of the whole business. In spite of Howe's incompetence in allowing Washington to slip through his fingers at Valley Forge and despite French naval and military support for the rebels, British forces managed to contain if not quite defeat the rebel armies. But the great disaster at Yorktown decided the issue when British Admiral Graves stupidly allowed the French fleet to slip in and take Cornwallis in the rear. After fighting for two weeks against impossible odds, on October 17, 1781, Cornwallis surrendered.

On September 3, 1783, the Treaty of Versailles was signed after prolonged scheming and negotiations at the French Court in which the British plenipotentiaries, Oswald and Vaughan, won the scorn of all students of diplomacy by their weak-kneed performance. John Adams, John Jay and Benjamin Franklin represented the United States. A more astute trio of diplomats would have been hard to find anywhere in Europe. Franklin wanted the entire continent turned over to the new republic. Even Lord Shelburne, the British prime minister, felt this was being a bit too open-handed. In the end the Americans settled in the west for the whole of the rich Ohio Valley—now Kentucky, Tennessee, Ohio, Alabama, Michigan, Wisconsin, Minnesota, Illinois and Indiana. In the east the British blundered also in defining the boundary line as the St. Croix River, thus inserting a wedge of alien territory between the present provinces of Quebec and New Brunswick.

The Loyalists

From 1775 those who had loyally supported the Crown were regarded as traitors by the new emerging state. In failing to hold the country for England they ended up by failing to hold anything for themselves. More than 30 loyalist American militia regiments fought against the rebel armies. Today such familiar names as the Loyal American Regiment, North Carolina Volunteers, New York Volunteers and the American Legion can trace their history to a time when they served as soldiers of the king.

Every form of penalty and persecution was imposed upon those who refused to support the republican cause—confiscation of property, tarring and feathering, houses and businesses burned to the ground, imprisonment and even death. On both sides, as feelings grew more bitter the treatment of noncombatants became more cruel. Thousands were driven from the country, from lands that their families had held for generations. Most were happy to escape with their lives. In 1784 the New York Legislature passed an act stating that any Loyalist found within the state who had taken part in the war "should be adjudged guilty of misprision of high treason." Sir Guy Carleton did everything possible to transport the suffering Loyalists to British territory before he evacuated New York.

Sir Frederick Haldimand, governor of Quebec, and John Parr of Nova Scotia did their best to receive and settle them on the vast vacant lands north of the border. They came flocking in the thousands to live under the flag they loved and served so well—in ships and in boats, in covered wagons and on foot.

Some 4500 settled along the shores of the St. Lawrence, 28,000 in what would become the Maritime provinces, several thousand in the Eastern Townships of Quebec and more than 10,000 in what would become the Province of Ontario. They came without money, with little food and few resources, with little knowledge of agriculture and an even smaller knowledge about the enormous hardships that faced them.

Theirs was not an exodus of some great horde of people unable to earn their living in a European country, ignorant, illiterate, uncultured and unprepared for the responsibilities of political life and the hardships of survival. It was a transfer of the prosperous upper class in the American community to a wilderness country. The Loyalists were the choicest stock the 13 colonies could boast. The undeniable brilliance of their leaders brought down the suspicion and wrath of the Sons of Liberty and those in the various state legislatures determined to purge the young republic of all dangerous elements and free thinkers.

The historian Hosmer wrote in his *Life of Henry Adams* that "the Tories were generally people of substance, their stake in the country was even greater than that of their opponents, their patriotism was no doubt to the full as fervent. The estates of the Tories were among the fairest, their stately mansions stood upon the sightliest hill-brow, the richest and best-tilled meadows were their farms." Of course not all of the 100,000 refugees were of this class nor did all of them move north to Canada. Some went to the West Indies or other colonies in Britain's far flung and growing empire. Others took up residence in England.

It was a migration without distinction of religion, occupation or ethnic considerations. They came bound by one ideal: their loyalty to the English Crown. Judges, lawyers, mechanics, craftsmen, farmers, soldiers, Catholics, Methodists, peaceful Pennsylvanian Quakers, and Mennonites. Even loyal Mohawk Indians led by Joseph Brant, survivors of the Six Nations, joined the northern migration and settled on the banks of the Thames River in what is today Brantford, Ontario.

Britain eventually decided to indemnify the Loyalists for actual losses incurred on behalf of the Crown. By 1790 Britain had paid out $19 million in

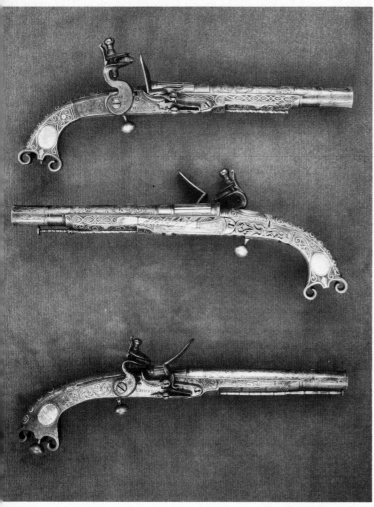

Flintlock pistols, c. 1790, made by John Murdoch of Scotland (active 1750-1798) and presented to William McGillvray, probably in 1804 when he became chief director of the North West Company.

claims—about $1.5 billion in today's dollars. The Loyalists received large land grants in every Province and in 1789 were given permission to use the title or affix by the Crown of "U.E.L." Every United Empire Loyalist and his or her descendants shared in this honour.

The Years of Consolidation

After the American Revolution Britain increased its Canadian defences and militia against the day that the Americans would try to take by force what Jay, Adams and Franklin had been unable to secure through negotiation. Halifax replaced Louisbourg as warden of the north. An uneasy peace settled over the continent.

Sir Guy Carleton, meanwhile, had become a peer of the realm. Lord Dorchester returned in 1786 as governor general of all British North America and at once perceived some modification was necessary to the Quebec Act that he had formulated. In 1791 the Province of Quebec was officially designated as Lower Canada while the English-speaking Loyalist areas to the west became Upper Canada.

Conditions in the two provinces were very different. The Upper Canadians, under Governor John Graves Simcoe, were British Loyalists trained in colonial self-government and firmly convinced of the fairness of British institutions. Simcoe, who had commanded the Queen's Rangers of Virginia during the Revolution, was one of those clear-sighted and determined characters so essential to the mould of nationality when success depends upon the initiative of those who possess authority.

Lower Canada, on the other hand, remained essentially French. It had a British governor, an assembly after the English pattern, the habeas corpus and criminal law of England, but little else. Lands were held through the old French feudal tenure, although to accommodate new settlers a freehold tenure was permitted by special request. French law prevailed in all civil matters together with French customs and language. The Catholic religion stood as the state church. The people were ignorant, untrained in constitutional matters and for several years unable to grasp the meaning of an elective assembly. When they did so the results were not exactly beneficial to themselves or the rest of the country.

The Maritime provinces were light years ahead of

their brethren as to the political awareness, wealth and culture. The first representative assembly on Canadian soil had been formed in Halifax back in 1758. Heavy British preferential duties in favour of lumber brought enormous wealth to the area; rivers were choked with floating timber and sawmills worked to capacity producing products for shipbuilding and manufacturing. The Duke of Kent's presence in Halifax as commander of forces in British America made that city a brilliant social centre, and the personal popularity of the future Queen Victoria's father caused the island of St. John to be renamed after Prince Edward.

When the French Revolution erupted in 1789 the U.S. professed itself sympathetic to its ideals although not towards the brutality by which they were carried out against the ruling classes. Although trade between American and British possessions along the Atlantic seaboard remained brisk, an underlying concern about the spirit of Yankee adventurism for territorial conquest was never far from anyone's mind.

In 1793 Britain joined Austria, the Dutch and Hanoverians and declared war against France. That same week in Nova Scotia Governor Sir John Wentworth ordered the formation of a militia regiment to consist of at least 600 men divided into six companies. By June, 800 had joined the popular Royal Nova Scotia Regiment. Its sister New Brunswick Regiment was never as popular and failed to reach its enlistment goal. Additional militia units were formed at Manchester, Lunenburg and Liverpool for harbour defences. In all Nova Scotia militia strength reached 9160, including one French Acadian force of 200 and a few unreliable companies of Micmac Indians. Most militia members were inadequately armed and badly provided.

During this latest British struggle with France, the U.S. claimed neutrality although it provided some aid to the chaotic political scene in France. In 1795 the American privateer schooner *La Solide* raided several Canadian coastal settlements. The militia was called out and in a quick exchange of fire defeated the Americans and seized the vessel. Napoleon Bonaparte, a 30-year-old artillery officer, took over the reins of French government in 1799 and embarked on his dramatic 10-year conquest of Europe. The Treaty of Amiens in 1809 briefly ended the war with France. The Canadian militia was

disbanded. After the short-lived peace both provincial militias were reformed as part of the British regular army into fencible (local territorial use only) regiments.

As the War of 1812 loomed Canada's population had grown to 100,000 in Upper Canada, 300,000 in Lower Canada and 100,000 in the Atlantic provinces, while the population in the United States had passed the 8 million mark.

The War of 1812

Britain and France's blockade of each other's seaports hurt the neutral powers, especially the new American republic. In 1805 Napoleon threatened to confiscate every neutral vessel calling at a British port. Two years later England decreed that all ships destined to French ports, or those of France's allies, visit a British port first and pay a cargo duty. Those that failed to comply were subject to confiscation. Vessels of trading nations that tried to abide by the rules of one country were automatically liable to seizure by the other.

Had there been any friendliness or kinship in the United States towards the mother country's struggle for the liberties of Europe, the blockade might have been accepted or modified through diplomatic negotiations. Except in parts of New England, these sentiments were generally lacking. Sufficient irritation still lingered from the day of the Revolution to feed the flames of outrage felt by American commercial interests over England's blockade.

Overseas, Britain struggled for national existence. Her very life depended upon the Royal Navy, whose strength was steadily being eroded by the desertion of its seaman to American vessels. Her right to search neutral ships on the high seas for deserters became the bone that stuck in the throat of American ship owners. On June 22, 1807 the British man of war HMS *Leopard* stopped the *Chesapeake*, an American 38-gun frigate, and demanded the return of four deserters. The American captain denied the presence of any deserters and refused to allow a British search party on board. A British salvo disabled the ship, killing or wounding 23 Americans. The British removed the four deserters plus three Americans whom they took to Halifax for trial. Later, Britain apologized for its high-handed action, returning two of the surviving Americans and recalling the officers responsible. But the damage was done. Three years later in an unprovoked attack an American frigate destroyed the British vessel *Little Belt*. Tit for tat.

Britain had no desire for further conflict and issued instructions to the governor general, Sir George Prevost, to do everything possible to appease the warhawks of the U.S. Congress. But the Americans wanted to round off the country with the acquisition of British North America and believed it could be had for the taking. Indeed, President Madison accepted renomination upon an actual pledge to declare war against England.

Napoleon had reached the zenith of his power with 400,000 of the finest troops ever trained by military genius at his disposal. Wellington's army was away fighting in the Peninsula while British money poured out like water trying to hold the allied nations of Europe from total collapse. The only remaining check on Napoleon's colossal ambitions came from the little island across the Channel against whom the United States declared war on June 18, 1812. At that moment Canada's continued existence seemed doomed.

Fewer than 5000 British troops stood spread along the 1200 miles of border line between Halifax and the Detroit River. The people of Upper Canada, where the bulk of the fighting would take place, numbered only 77,000. There were few roads. Indian footpaths connected most of the tiny settlements overland. The country's defence was inferior to the Americans' in every respect except for the British ships cruising the Great Lakes. The Americans had nothing to equal them. So certain was former President Thomas Jefferson of the result that he described the anticipated American victory as "a mere matter of marching." Eustis, President Madison's secretary of war, declared that "we can take Canada without soldiers." War-hawk Congressman Henry Clay announced that "we have the Canadas as much under our command as she (England) has the ocean."

Much of the success of the provinces in resisting the invasion of their territories by 11 different American armies in the ensuing two years was the result of the courage and wisdom of Maj.-Gen. Sir Isaac Brock, the army commander and lieutenant governor of Upper Canada. When word reached Brock through a private source of the American declaration, he knew that everything depended on swift and sweep-

ing action. Immediately he sent some British regulars to try to hold the Niagara frontier, called out the militia and summoned the Legislature, pending official instructions from Governor General Prevost.

While he waited, American Gen. Hull crossed the St. Clair River from Detroit on July 11 with 2500 men and issued a flamboyant proclamation giving protection to all noncombatants and declaring that the imminent conquest would provide relief from British "tyranny and oppression." He promised "instant destruction" of all who were captured fighting beside the Indians. Brock, realizing how important his Indian allies would be, promptly sent a force to attack Michilimackinac, in what is now northern Michigan. Its American commander, unaware the two countries were at war, surrendered. The Indians were mightily impressed and thereafter, under their chief Tecumseh, threw their support completely with the British. At the news of Michilimackinac Hull retired with his forces across the river to Detroit.

A week later Brock, with 320 regulars and 400 militia from York and Lincoln and assisted by Tecumseh and 600 of his Indians, crossed the St. Clair in pursuit of the enemy. Hull was startled by a terse summons to surrender in which Brock warned of the difficulty he would have controlling his Indian contingent once the battle started. Nervously Hull watched the little force cross the river, Gen. Brock "erect in his canoe, leading the way to battle," as Tecumseh later described the event. Terrified at the prospect of slaughter by Tecumseh's Indians, Hull's imagination got the best of him. Before a shot could be fired from either side he surrendered his entire force, including the 4th United States Regiment and its colours.

This capitulation delivered to Brock the entire Michigan Territory, including the town and port of Detroit, which commanded the whole of western Canada. Included in the spoils were the American brig *Adams*, 33 cannons and a huge supply of arms, stores, weapons and gunpowder. Brock's bold attack set the stage for the entire subsequent struggle. It inspired the militia in every province, electrified the masses with fresh determination to beat the invader and suppressed any disloyal tendencies among resident American sympathizers.

The American battle plan involved moving 8000 troops to the border crossing at Niagara. After taking Queenston Heights they planned to overrun the province with troops brought at leisure from their immense reserves. Simultaneously, Gen. Dearborn with a large force was to march on Montreal from New York by way of Lake Champlain; Gen. Harrison would invade Upper Canada from Michigan with 6000 men, while Commodore Chauncey took a force across Lake Ontario.

Operations began on October 13 with an attempt to move 1500 regulars and 2500 militia across the Niagara River. About 1100 troops, followed slowly by other detachments, succeeded in crossing and climbed Queenston Heights against light resistance from the British outpost and took the battery. Meantime, Brock—now Sir Isaac Brock (he had been gazetted a Knight of the Bath the week before)— arrived from his post at nearby Fort George. But before he could do anything more than show himself to his troops and shout "Push on the York Volunteers!" he fell with a ball through his chest. His second-in-command, Lieutenant-Colonel John McDonell, attorney-general of the province, led a second charge up the hill. He too died in the attempt.

Reinforcements under Maj.-Gen. Sheaffe arrived a short time later and in a flanking movement charged with 800 men. Already harassed by the Indians, the Americans were dislodged from the Heights after the first volley. In their headlong retreat many were dashed to pieces on the rocks or drowned attempting to swim the river. When reinforcements from the New York militia failed to cross the river, the remaining 960 Americans surrendered, including a major-general, six colonels and 56 other officers.

The Americans made a few half-hearted attempts to take Kingston and Montreal before suspending operations for the winter. Against all odds the Canadians had proved they could they defend themselves and they were now in control of large parts of Michigan and the territories west of Lake Erie.

The campaign of 1813 was not quite so spectacular although it began well. In January, Col. Procter, with 500 British regulars and 800 Indians under the Wyandotte chief Roundhead, crossed the frozen St. Clair River and attacked Gen. Winchester. After a sharp battle the Americans surrendered. Procter moved next against Fort Meigs with 900 men and 1200 Indians. Although he defeated the American ground forces he was unable to take the fort. During

Royal Ontario Museum, Toronto

A bullet mould from the first half of the 19th century. Soft lead was squeezed between the pincers to obtain the proper calibre.

Maj.-Gen. Sir Isaac Brock (1769-1812) arrived in Canada from the West Indies in 1802. His bold defence saved Upper Canada from falling into the hands of the Americans in the War of 1812.

Zebulon Montgomery Pike (after whom Pike's Peak in the American Rockies was named) and for some time were held in check by the determined resistance of two companies of the 8th Regiment and 200 militiamen. The fort, some distance from the town itself, was captured finally after the accidental explosion of a powder magazine in which Pike and 260 of his men were killed. Gen. Sheaffe withdrew his small force of regulars from York and retreated to Kingston. The town surrendered and despite the terms of capitulation was promptly pillaged and all its public buildings burned. The church was robbed of its plate and the legislative library looted.

Next, the Americans moved against Fort George on the Niagara frontier. British Gen. Vincent put up a stubborn defence but was finally forced to retreat. The Americans entered the fort on May 27. Thereafter, U.S. spirits were dampened by heavy rains and a flood of contradictory orders from their commander, Dearborn. A week passed before the Americans took up the pursuit. Col. Harvey, a brilliant soldier of the Brock mould and later lieutenant governor of the Maritime provinces, attacked a large force of 3500 Americans encamped at Burlington Heights (near Hamilton) during the night of June 5. Two American generals and over a hundred other ranks were taken together with a number of guns. This victory was followed by the British defeat on Lake Erie of Captain Barclay, who with six ships and 300 seamen was resoundingly beaten by nine of Commodore Perry's vessels and twice the number of men.

Even more disastrous and disgraceful was Gen. Procter's conduct in October. Fearing a counterattack, he made a rapid withdrawal towards Burlington Heights. Tecumseh, commanding the Indian force and always ready to fight the Americans, compared Procter to "a whipped dog crawling away with its tail between its legs." Procter fell back along the Thames River with 800 of Tecumseh's Indians and 400 troops, many of them sick. Gen. Harrison's American force of 3500 men caught up with Procter at Moraviantown on October 5 and defeated him. The gallant Tecumseh fell during the battle; 290 of Procter's troops escaped to Ancaster while the rest were taken prisoner. Procter disgraced himself by fleeing the field early in the encounter. He was later court-martialed, censured and deprived of command for six months.

the ensuing siege the Indians, bored by this form of inactive warfare, drifted away "leaving me with less than 20 chiefs and Warriors." Western Indian reinforcements enabled Procter to try an attack against Fort Stevenson. However, once again he was unable to get through the American defenses.

Further east, Col. George McDonell attacked Ogdensburg, New York in late February, capturing 11 guns, a large quantity of ordinance, military stores and two armed schooners. Seventy-four officers and men were taken prisoner. The Americans evened the score in April when Commodore Chauncey with a fleet of 14 ships and 1700 troops sailed from Sackett's Harbor on the New York side of Lake Ontario to York (later Toronto), then a small settlement of 800 and containing the provincial seat of government. The Americans landed under Brig.

The greatest loss to the Canadians was Tecumseh. Territory could always be recaptured, but the great Indian leader was gone. He was a savage of the heroic mould who, when acting with men like Brock, was almost invincible. His Indians would do anything for him—even refraining from massacre or cruelty. The Americans amply demonstrated their fear of him by the indignities they inflicted upon his corpse.

By October an American army of 8000 men had assembled at Sackett's Harbor, New York, under Gens. Boyd and Wilkinson. They planned to attack Lower Canada by floating down the St. Lawrence River to Montreal. A small body of British troops, accompanied by eight gunboats and three field pieces, pursued them, inflicting considerable damage. On November 11, Wilkinson and his main army with the flotilla were near Prescott, moving to join Gen. Hampton's army at the mouth of the Chateauguay River for the advance on Montreal. Boyd, with 2500 men, marched along the shore harried by 800 troops under Col. Morrison who decided to overtake and attack him at Crysler's Farm.

In the resulting battle, one of the most complete Canadian victories of the war, the Americans were routed with the loss of 339 officers and men to Morrison's 181. Gen. Boyd immediately returned with what remained of his baggage and troops to the boats and joined Wilkinson. Together, they continued downriver to join Hampton.

Hampton, meanwhile, had been marching with his 7000 men from Lake Champlain to the mouth of the Chateauguay. During the night of October 25, in dense forest, he came against Col. de Salaberry and 300 French-Canadian militiamen with a few Indians and supported by Col. McDonell with another French contingent of 600 men who had made the most rapid overland forced march in Canadian history and reached Chateauguay the day before the battle. The Americans advanced with 4000 men against the first line of hidden defenders. As they drove them back they met the second line under Col. McDonell.

McDonell had placed his buglers a considerable distance apart in the woods. The call to attack given on these instruments when mixed with the bloodthirsty yells and war cries of some 50 scattered Indians scared the wits out of Hampton's men, who were convinced they were outnumbered and about to be slaughtered. They fled into the darkness. Hampton's failure to meet Wilkinson and Boyd's forces at Chateauguay ended any further American thoughts of capturing Montreal. The clever stratagem by 2000 brilliantly commanded Canadian and British troops had succeeded in defeating 15,000 incompetently led Americans. The only sour note to the campaign was Governor General Prevost's attempt in his despatches to claim the entire credit for victory to himself. But the facts became known, largely because of the intervention by the Duke of Kent, a friend of De Salaberry. Both De Salaberry and McDonell were decorated after the war.

Upper Canada was also treated to an example of Prevost's embarrassing military incompetence. Frightened by Procter's defeat near Moraviantown, he ordered Gen. Vincent, the British commander at Burlington and York, to abandon his posts and withdraw down the lake to Kingston. Fortunately Vincent was made of sterner stuff than the governor general. "That man Prevost is a fool!" he observed and held his ground. Col. Murray with 378 regulars, a few volunteers and some Indians led by Tecumseh's brother, Tenkswatawa, were given permission to advance against the enemy at Fort George, where Gen. McClure and 2700 Americans were camped. McClure, radically overestimating the attacking force, withdrew on December 10 after burning to the ground the nearby village of Newark, one-time capital of Upper Canada. The wanton and tactically pointless destruction of this pretty village on a bitterly cold winter's night achieved nothing. The male inhabitants were either away fighting or already prisoners of the Americans. Those remaining were old people, women and children. They were forced out into the snow in whatever clothes they were wearing. British retribution was swift. The American Fort Niagara, just across the river, was promptly stormed and held until the end of the war. The neighbouring villages of Lewiston, Youngstown, Manchester and Tuscarora were burned.

This ended the campaign for 1813. During two years the Americans had achieved little; not only had they been consistently beaten in every encounter by forces vastly inferior in numbers but they had lost all the benefits of Harrison's success against the incompetent Procter as well as Fort Niagara. After all their efforts, only Amherstburg on the Upper Canadian frontier remained in their possession.

The last campaign of the war began in Lower Canada with another advance from Lake Champlain by Gen. Wilkinson and 4000 troops. A Canadian force of 300 men led by Maj. Handcock checked the American advance at Lacolle's Mill, a small stone building on the Lacolle River between Plattsburg and Montreal. The Americans withdrew.

In Upper Canada, Gen. Sir Gordon Drummond, a brave and capable officer, became army commander. After the spring ice breakup he sent Col. McDonell with a relief force to Michilimackinac to thwart any plans the Americans might have for retaking their strategic waterway into Lake Michigan. In May, Drummond and Sir James Yeo, the naval commander, captured Fort Oswego on the New York side of Lake Ontario with all its supplies and stores.

Early in July American Maj.-Gen. Brown, with 5000 troops backed by 4000 New York militia, invaded Upper Canada from Buffalo. To meet this threat Drummond had fewer than 4000 regulars. Prevost, frightened by the American forces massed at Lake Champlain, turned a deaf ear to Drummond's requests for reinforcements. As a result Fort Erie surrendered to the Americans on July 3 and Gen. Riall was defeated at Chippewa two days later with the loss of 511 men. Unchecked, the Americans continued their advance.

On July 25, Drummond arrived at the scene from Kingston with 800 men and assumed command. At Lundy's Lane, within the sound of Niagara Falls, the fiercest battle of the war was fought well into the night. When it ended both sides claimed victory. After trying for six hours with 5000 men to force Drummond's position with half that number, Brown withdrew to Chippewa after losing 930 men to Drummond's 870. The following day he retreated to Fort Erie where, after an unsuccessful attack by Drummond for the loss of 500 troops, he remained bottled up inside the fort until September.

With the war in Europe temporarily over, 16,000 experienced British troops were despatched to Quebec. Prevost advanced on Plattsburg with 12,000 of these soldiers, where he planned to attack in conjunction with the British fleet on Lake Champlain. However, when the fleet went down to defeat, Prevost shamefully withdrew his force in the face of 2500 Americans troops. Later recalled by London for

cowardice, he managed to escape the condemnation of a court martial by conveniently dying. In spite of Prevost's disgraceful conduct, the year ended with the Americans in control only of Lake Erie, while Canadian forces held Lake Ontario, several forts on American soil and a substantial portion of the state of Maine.

The lieutenant governor of Nova Scotia, Maj.-Gen. Sir John Sherbrooke, using a force of regular troops together with ships of the Royal Navy based in Halifax, had made a series of attacks along the Maine coast and frontier during 1814. The resulting successes placed the entire region from Penobscot to the St. Croix River in Canadian hands. Although Sherbrooke had been sending troops up to Canada whenever they became were available, the war never affected the Maritime provinces with the same severity as the rest of the country.

Elsewhere on land and sea the conflict had been equally varied. Both England and America won their share of naval victories. A purely British part of the struggle included the capture of Washington and the burning of its public buildings in revenge for the incineration of York and Newark and the American conduct along the Niagara frontier. An attempt in January 1815 to capture New Orleans ended in disaster with over 2500 British troops killed, wounded or missing. Worse, the terrible bloodshed was all for nothing. A peace had been signed on Christmas Eve a month earlier. Ironically, the two issues of right of search and the position of neutrals during time of war were not even mentioned in the Treaty of Ghent.

Since the Americans won the last battle they quite naturally claimed final victory. However, for all their slaughtered citizenry and flag waving they had gained not a foot of Canadian territory nor a single political or sentimental advantage from the conflict. Their capital city had been partially destroyed, their annual exports were reduced almost to zero and their merchant class nearly ruined. The huge war tax levied in New England angered residents for decades thereafter. If the conflict produced any winners they had to be the 500,000 Canadians and few British troops who, after three years of often bloody conflict against overwhelming odds with a nation of 8 million, had emerged territorially intact and convinced of their decision to remain loyal to the British Crown.

"Fort Erie. Defence of the Block House." The Americans defend their prize against Drummond's attack, July 26, 1814.

(Overleaf)
The Battle of Queenston Heights. In the foreground the dying Brock delivers his final words: "Push on, York Volunteers!"

"Tecumseh defends the Whites at Fort Meigs."

"Battle of the Thames 5th Oct 1813. Respectfully dedicated to the Real Hero Col. Richard M. Johnson Vice President of the United States." In the centre of this American lithograph Col. Johnson fights with Tecumseh and the Indian chief receives the pistol shots that took his life.

"Macdonough's Victory on Lake Champlain, and Defeat
of the British Army at Plattsburg by Genl. Macomb, Septr.
11th 1814."

"Engagement in the Thousand Islands," a coloured
lithograph after Coke Smyth.

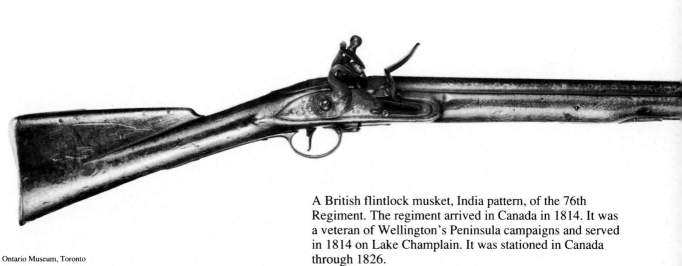

A British flintlock musket, India pattern, of the 76th
Regiment. The regiment arrived in Canada in 1814. It was
a veteran of Wellington's Peninsula campaigns and served
in 1814 on Lake Champlain. It was stationed in Canada
through 1826.

23rd and 24th Nov. 1837."

REBELS AND RAIDERS

At the conclusion of hostilities the warships on the Great Lakes were slowly disassembled. Canada and the U.S. agreed to one vessel each on Lakes Champlain and Ontario and two on the upper Great Lakes. Nova Scotia's defences were rebuilt. The Halifax Citadel was refurbished and became one of the strongest fortresses of its day. Fortifications at Quebec and Montreal were also improved with new guns and supply depots, although the defences of both towns remained as inadequate as they had been during the war.

In Upper Canada, plans were made to strengthen Kingston with a system of supporting forts. To counter any further American attempts to cut the St. Lawrence River lifeline to Montreal, the Rideau Canal system was constructed. Although the Rideau system was completed, the grandiose plans for Kingston ended with the construction of Fort Henry. Two decades passed. Prospects for a renewed American invasion faded to be replaced by a series of divisive internal grumblings in both Upper and Lower Canada. "The Troubles of 1837-38," as they came to be known to the Colonial Office in London, were the first birth pains of a free government in Canada.

In England, the shy and diminutive 18-year-old Alexandrina Victoria, daughter of Edward, Duke of Kent, ascended the throne she was to hold for the next 64 years. The British Empire approached the zenith of its global power and political influence. With the exception of Prussia and Austria, Germany remained no more than a collection of fractious autocratic states. Imperial Russia, under the conservative Czar Nicholas I, languished in a bureaucratic backwater—a fairyland of indolence and leisure for the privileged few—tyrannical serfdom for the majority.

Canada's troubles came about through a combination of spellbinding oratory and armed rebellion by an agitated few anxious to discard the less admirable aspects of British colonial rule and assert a republican style of independence. The Lower Canada Rebellion was centred in Montreal. Louis-Joseph Papineau, who led the "Patriotes" of Lower Canada, demanded nothing less than self-government based on the French-Canadian majority. Fighting broke out on November 6, 1837, between the militant French-speaking Sons of Liberty and the equally militant English-speaking Doric Club. British military and militia pickets surrounded Montreal while the Royal Artillery paraded in the streets. Unofficial military drills by the militia were forbidden. By the following week an arrest warrant had been issued for Papineau and the other French leaders. Troops sent out to bring them in were met by armed rioters and forced to retreat to avoid bloodshed.

News of the uprising spread. Outside Montreal in the villages of St. Denis and St. Charles armed groups organized under Papineau. Sir John Colborne, general of all Lower Canada forces, ordered troops to both locations to put down the insurrection. On November 22, the force sent against St. Denis under Col. Gore was forced to retreat after several hours of fighting. Meanwhile, Lieut.-Col. Weatherell easily occupied St. Charles, scattering its defenders.

Gore's second attempt to take St. Denis a week later was successful. His troops set fire to the Patriotes' homes after discovering the mutilated

(Overleaf)
"Attack on St. Charles, 23rd 24th Nov. 1837."

Royal Ontario Museum, Toronto

remains of a cavalry officer who had been captured on the road from Montreal and hacked to pieces. The Patriotes fled to the United States. News of the first success against Gore reached the townspeople of St. Eustache. Four hundred of them under Dr. Chenier broke into the government armoury, took what weapons they could find and marched through the streets, helping themselves to whatever liquor was available along the way. Colborne moved 2000 troops to St. Eustache to meet this new threat. The Patriotes retreated to a church and prepared their defence. Colborne bombarded the church first then rushed it, setting fire to what remained of the structure. Over 70 of the Patriotes were killed and 120 taken prisoner.

Two months later, on the last day of February 1838, a force claiming to represent the "Republic of Lower Canada" under the leadership of Robert Nelson and Dr. Côté marched against Montreal. Finding their way barred by Loyalist Mississquoi Militia, they retreated to the U.S. and surrendered their arms. Determined to try again the rebels reorganized at Napierville and on November 4, Nelson was proclaimed president of the new republic. A call to arms went out and 2500 men assembled. Unfortunately only 250 muskets could be found to equip this enthusiastic force of rebels.

To solve the problem Dr. Côté set off to capture more arms for the "Republic." On his way to Rouse's Point he met and easily defeated a force of Loyalist militia at LaColle. However, on his return march, the LaColle militia had been reinforced. Côté was defeated and his men dispersed leaving "President" Nelson and the remaining 1000 faithful to beat a speedy retreat towards the U.S. They were surrounded at Odelltown by a militia force and Nelson fled across the border alone. The Lower Canada rebellions were over.

The Upper Canada rebellion under William Lyon Mackenzie proved to be even more of a farce than its counterpart under Papineau. Mackenzie lacked both Papineau's organization and oratory skills. In 1836 Mackenzie tried to reorganize the disintegrating Reform Party, which for years had been advocating political change to the Upper Canada Legislature. His attempts were met with catcalls of "treason," fistfights and showers of stones. Party members began arming themselves and attending regular training drills on weaponry and marching.

Upper Canada's Lieutenant Governor Francis Bond Head dismissed any idea of a rebel attack against Toronto. When word of the Lower Canada rebellion reached him he sent all available troops to assist. With half the troops away in Quebec, Mackenzie decided to attack, demanding a fair assembly or, if refused, independence. After a week of postponements 800 poorly equipped and exhausted men arrived to go out and do battle. Many who turned up from outlying villages and farms left immediately after seeing the condition of Mackenzie's pathetic little force and its lack of arms. One disillusioned rebel who went home wrote that Mackenzie "spends his time shouting, swearing and raving like a lunatic."

The lieutenant governor was warned by a Loyalist militiaman in plenty of time to meet the threat and the city's bells rang out a call for the general population to take up arms. On the evening of December 5, 1836, Mackenzie's force appeared marching cautiously down Yonge Street. A half mile from the city they met the loyalists. Both sides exchanged musket fire and ran in opposite directions. At the first volley Mackenzie bolted like a rabbit. Two days later he tried again; but many of his supporters had left. Militia reinforcements meanwhile were pouring into Toronto from across the province. The rebels panicked and ran. Mackenzie, with a £1000 price on his head and in the best tradition of other Canadian traitors, fled to the U.S., where he set up a political headquarters on Navy Island above Niagara Falls. He was eventually arrested in the U.S. and sentenced to 18 months imprisonment by a jury in Albany, New York.

For two more years conspiracies in various American cities continued to support the Canadian rebels through so-called Hunter's Lodges. These groups organized and drilled large bodies of men and, at different times and places, invaded Canada. Fortunately, this desultory guerrilla warfare lacked organization and a leader with brains. In most cases the sight of a Canadian militia force was sufficient to send the enthusiastic raiders scampering back across the border.

At Prescott, near Kingston, a band of rebel raiders under Von Schultz, a Polish refugee, were captured after a spirited battle with British and Canadian troops. In the trial that followed Von Schultz was defended by a young lawyer, John A. Macdonald.

The case was Macdonald's first. He lost. Von Schultz and eleven of his followers were convicted and hanged.

The last of the "Troubles" ended in December 1839 when a band of 450 rebel raiders was cheered through the streets of Detroit on its way to capture Windsor. They crossed the river, took the town and burned a vessel and a few houses. A small guard of Canadian militia was captured. When one of its members refused to join the rebel ranks, he was murdered.

The raiders marched on to the village of Sandwich, where they ran into Col. John Prince, a stern no-nonsense Loyalist, leading a detachment of 200 militiamen. In a quick exchange of musketry Prince routed the rebels. When he discovered the wanton murder of the local surgeon by the retreating mob, he ordered four prisoners to the front and, in swift retribution, had them shot. Two of the rebel leaders—Lount and Matthews—who failed to make it back to the States were later tried, convicted and executed.

The result of the rebellions was a renewed interest in military protection for the country. The force of British regulars was increased to 8000 and the militia strengthened. Five new militia battalions were created and stationed around Hamilton, Cornwall and Prescott. Provincial cavalry and artillery units were also formed together with a company of Negroes known as the Brantford Light Infantry. In 1840 the Royal Canadian Rifles was created. Made up of veterans with seven years of service, its duty was to defend Canada's frontier posts. Because many of its enlisted members were married, wives were given free rations and provided with married quarters; this political decision was designed to attract experienced soldiers and persuade them to remain in a peacetime army. The Royal Canadian Rifles remained active until 1870, providing a cadre of first-class instructors for Canada's militia units.

The Coming of Age, 1840-1867.

In 1840 Upper and Lower Canada were united into one nation with a militia force capable of mustering over 200,000 troops. The numbers were deceptive. Most units were neither operational nor equipped with suitable weaponry. The regular militia training musters gradually turned into social events, sometimes ending in drunken brawls and deaths.

Britain grew tired of paying for Canada's defence. In 1846 it began bringing its troops home or sending them for service elsewhere in the Empire. During the Crimean War between Russia and England, British troops in Canada and the Maritimes were reduced to 3300. Canada was given the task of organizing its own defence requirements. After considerable argument a new Militia Act was passed in 1855 dividing Canada into 18 military districts, each commanded by a colonel with the necessary staff. Military districts were subdivided into units or "companies." Commanding officers were responsible for enrolment. Overall militia command became the responsibility of the adjutant general and his two deputies.

Known as the volunteer "Active Militia," it became enormously popular partly because of the payment of 5 to 10 shillings per day for serving members. The ceiling of 5000 men was quickly passed and the government was forced to amend the act to include unpaid volunteers. Arrangements were made to raise a force of Canadian regulars to serve with the British. Although England could no longer demand Canadian recruits, it could ask for volunteers.

A number of Canadians answered when Britain sent out a call for volunteers during the troubles in India. The Canadian government created the 100th Royal Canadian Regiment of Foot in 1858, which

A wooden powder keg, 19th century. It could be carried by one man comfortably.   Royal Ontario Museum, Toronto

49

became the first unit raised in Canada to serve abroad. However, it soon became apparent to the Colonial Office in London that Canadian forces were simply too weak to defend the country's borders against American incursions. British troops were despatched again to Canada.

The Americans were becoming bolder. President James Buchanan commanded a nation on the verge of civil war. Washington and the Northern States believed Southern Seccessionist spies lurked everywhere. In 1861 the U.S. Navy stopped a British vessel on the high seas and seized two Confederate agents. Tensions were high. England sent more troops to Canada. In the summer of '62 there were 18,000 British regulars in the country. New volunteers flocked to the militia units. A government bill expanding the militia to 50,000 men was defeated by the opposition.

The success of the U.S. Northern Armies caused some adjustment to the perceived threat over the border. Nevertheless, the number of militia volunteers was increased to 35,000 and two military schools were opened. The schools became so popular that a provision was made later for four more. During the American Civil War Canadian sympathies lay with the Southern Confederacy and Northerners fumed when many escaping Confederate prisoners of war found refuge in Canada.

In 1862 a British commission concluded that it would take 150,000 troops to defend Canada and then only if fortifications and communications were considerably improved. Between 1865 and 1872 an unenthusiastic Britain spent £249,454 to construct three redoubts opposite Quebec City. The danger passed. The U.S. did not attack. The war ended. The huge Northern army demobilized and went home, but a new threat appeared.

The American Fenian Brotherhood was a band of Irish nationalist revolutionaries dedicated to ending British rule of Ireland. The American Fenians, led by John O'Mahony, consisted mainly of embittered immigrants who had fled Ireland during the potato famines and after the 1848 rebellion against England. O'Mahony's original intention was to raise money for shipping guns and supplies to Ireland. This was abandoned in favour of an armed invasion of Canada. Demobilized U.S. soldiers provided excellent trained recruits. By early spring in 1866 as many as 35,000 Fenian troops were secretly positioned at various towns along the U.S.-Canadian border. To counter the Fenian threat Canada had called 20,000 militiamen to arms.

The first Fenian raid took place in New Brunswick. Swift action by the local militia, British warships and the American authorities prevented any serious conflict in what turned out to be a half-hearted affair. Quantities of arms and ammunition were seized by the Americans and a number of Fenian officers arrested. But the action so frightened the people of New Brunswick that they became ardent supporters of Canadian Confederation the following year. The Fenian raid along the Niagara was a more serious business. This attack, launched on June 6 , 1866 and led by John O'Neill, a former Union Army officer, was supposedly part of a larger invasion force. Crossing the Niagara with 800 men to the cheers of American spectators lining the American side of the river, O'Neill captured Fort Erie. At the battle of Ridgeway, fought later on the same day, O'Neill and his force withdrew back to the U.S. where they promptly surrendered to the U.S. Navy on board the gunboat USS *Michigan*. The U.S. government paid their railway tickets home.

In spite of the enthusiasm of the Canadian Militia during the Fenian border skirmishes, supplies, rations, transport and staff problems nearly ended defensive operations before they began. The last Fenian attack took place in 1870 along the Quebec border. The force was met by militia cavalry and infantry from Montreal. In the face of a swift Canadian advance, the Fenian army disintegrated and fled across the border, where its leaders were arrested by the U.S. authorities.

In the aftermath of the Fenian raids the militia was severely criticized for its misuse of cavalry and lack of training. Efforts were taken at once to improve this situation. More money and newer weapons were approved. The Thorold Training Camp for Infantry was created and a similar camp planned at Toronto. Field brigades were organized with a mix of 500 regulars and 1000 volunteers supported by small cavalry and artillery units. And, for the first time, a medical formation with a surgeon and medical officers in a ratio of 1-400 came into being.

"Front View of the Church of St. Eustache Occupied by
the Insurgents. The Artillery Forcing an Entrance. 14th
Dec. 1837."

PAC C8338

Ontario Archives

(Facing page)
(Top) The Prince Consort's Own Rifle Brigade at Grimsby, Ont., out for rifle practice, 1862. (Below) Officers at annual militia camp, Laprairie, Que., 1863.

(Overleaf)
An American lithograph showing the "Battle of Ridgeway, C.W. Desperate Charge of the Fenians, under Col. O'Neill, near Ridgeway Station, June 2, 1866, and Total Rout of the British Troops, including the Queen's Own Regt under Command of Col. Booker."

Royal Ontario Museum, Toronto

Oxford Militia on Perry Street, Woodstock, 1865.

Ontario Archives

"Action Near Freleysburg. Precipitate retreat of the British
Vol. Cavalry, 99 strong, near Freleysburg, Canada East, on
the 8th of June 1866, when charged by Major P. O'Hara,
with 15 men of the 3rd Mass. Infantry, Army of Ireland,
F.B. The enemy left their flag in the hands of their
wounded Standard bearer, which was afterwards brought
to New York and trailed to the hearse of an Irish Soldier
who died at Malone."

(Facing page)
Elora Volunteer Militia Rifle Company, 1866, and (below)
troops leaving Prescott, Canada West, in June 1866.

Sappers at work levelling a recreation ground, Esquimalt, B.C., c.1870.

CONFEDERATION

On July 1, 1867, Canada became one nation with Nova Scotia and New Brunswick. Conservative Sir John A. Macdonald headed the nation's first constitutionally elected government. National defence became a main concern. £1,100,000 was authorized for fortifications. However, steadily improving relations with the U.S. caused the money to be transferred to railway construction. A new Federal Militia Act was passed providing an active militia strength of 40,000 volunteers. Active militia units were given 16 days training annually. The country was redivided into nine military districts. Provision was made also for a reserve militia of all males from the age of 18 to 60 but this was purely a paper force.

The first foreign service by Canadian volunteers came a year after Confederation when a force of 500 men was raised and sent to Italy to defend the Pope against Garibaldi. Known as the Canadian Pontifical Zouaves, they put up only a token resistance before returning to Canada the following year. By 1870 there were 37,170 officers and men in the active militia.

In February the British government advised Canada that it would be taking the bulk of its troops home. Her Majesty's government was no longer willing to spend money on defending an independent colony. Halifax would be left as the only remaining garrison of Imperial troops on the continent. Happily, these British withdrawals coincided with a new peace treaty with the U.S.

The reconstituted Canadian militia went into action immediately in the Red River settlement of Manitoba, where Métis settlers were unhappy about the government taking away their lands. The Métis had formed a provisional government under Louis Riel and threatened trouble. On May 25, 1870, two battalions of militia recruited for one year were sent to relieve Imperial troops already in Manitoba. Transport of the expeditionary force sent out under command of Col. Garnet J. Wolseley was made difficult because the Americans would not allow armed Canadians to be transported over their railways or canals systems. Overland Canadian routes were poor to nonexistent. Wolseley's force made 47 portages before reaching Fort Garry. It rained for seven of the 13 weeks that the men were in transit, and no one had been issued with proper rainwear. Wolseley arrived at Fort Garry on August 24 to relieve the British troops. His men were rewarded with all the whisky available in Winnipeg. Four days later the British departed for Montreal over the same route.

To compensate for this loss of British expertise and influence the government organized two batteries of artillery in Kingston and Quebec that doubled as gunnery schools. When the Liberal opposition defeated Sir John A. Macdonald's Conservatives, military expenses were pared by two thirds to offset a current North American economic depression. No new camps were formed and training was severely curtailed. The only two bright spots during the austerity period were the formation of the North West Mounted Police and the creation of the Royal Military College at Kingston. The college opened on June 1, 1876, to 18 cadets. Its four-year course concentrated on both civil and military skills. It enjoyed great success, eventually becoming a rival to the U.S. West Point. Yet in spite of the cutbacks and impoverished condition of the militia the government had to call out the force to put down public riots in Montreal and Quebec.

PAC PA88283

Gatling gun, c.1880. This is an early version, in which the barrels were arrayed in a row, instead of the more familiar cylindrical shape. Patented by American inventor Richard Gatling in 1862, it first saw service in the U.S. Civil War. Eight to ten barrels were used.

In 1877 Russia attacked Turkey and continued its advance into the Middle East. British authorities became alarmed. Rumours blossomed on all sides. In Canada word came that a Russian warship had appeared off the east coast ready to bombard Halifax; an entire Russian fleet was reported to be preparing support for a series of landings along the West Coast from San Francisco to British Columbia. The Canadian government panicked. As if by magic, funds for immediate and wholesale defence improvements reappeared. Yet the vulnerability of the West Coast remained a nagging concern for both Liberal and successive Conservative governments, and although a few rudimentary defences were subsequently built, no real and permanent steps were taken in this direction until 1893.

A long report from the commander of the militia to the government in 1880 outlined the country's military shortages and need for improvements. Someone in Ottawa listened and a few hesitant steps were taken. A smooth-bore gun was converted to a rifled barrel.

Consideration was given to switching over all guns and refitting them with sights and breech-loading shells. The idea was dropped as too expensive. Instead, a central government arsenal for maintaining the inventory of outdated guns and ammunition was created.

In 1883 a new militia act authorized a permanent Canadian armed force of one cavalry troop, three batteries of militia and three companies of infantry. Troops were limited to 750 men, later raised to 1000. Hardly a force to be reckoned with in a nation now approaching four and a half million population. There was much public opposition to such a permanent armed force. A suspicious militia believed all government defence money would go to the new force. A suspicious electorate worried over the additional taxes to pay for it and the possibility of a military coup by its idle senior officers. The fears turned out to be unfounded. Most members of the new force were kept busy with administrative and instructional duties and apparently had little time or inclination to organize a military takeover. The public relaxed, paid the tax increase and two years later congratulated itself on having had the foresight to provide a cadre of trained career soldiers to combat the Riel Rebellion.

The Northwest Rebellion

Louis Riel reappeared after his banishment of 1870 and began organizing a provisional Métis government. On March 2, 1885, Riel and 40 men seized the mailbags and courier's horses at Duck Lake in the territory of what is now the province of Saskatchewan, 300 miles north of the path of the Canadian Pacific Railway. Riel invited the surrounding Indian settlements to join the new government. Sedition turned to armed rebellion at the Battle of Duck Lake on March 25 when a band of Métis under Gabriel Dumont fired on a party of North-West Mounted Police under Maj. Crozier who were attempting to obtain supplies. Crozier's force fought back but was defeated with a loss of 11 dead and many more wounded. If the gallant major had had the patience to wait an extra two hours, substantial reinforcements would have arrived on the scene.

Riel's victory brought him many Indian allies. They began to raid and loot Battleford, eventually occupying the entire town with the exception of the police barracks. Farther west, Cree Indians attacked Frog

Lake and the lightly defended Fort Pitt, forcing a wholesale evacuation. The Indians stormed into the fort, took everything of value, then burned it to the ground. The government acted quickly, mobilizing 7982 officers and men from as far away as Halifax. The troops were divided into three columns and gathered at different points along the uncompleted railway line from where they marched north to the troubled areas. As in 1870, the Americans refused permission for armed men to pass through their territory, which resulted in much hardship and suffering by the men.

Artillery Lieut.-Col. C.E. Montizambert described part of the trip: "About 400 miles had to be passed by constantly varying process of embarking and disembarking guns and stores from flat cars to country team sleighs and vice versa. There were 16 operations of this nature in cold weather and deep snow. On starting from the west end of the track... the roads were found so bad that it took the guns 17 hours to do the distance (30 miles) to Magpie Camp. On from there to the east end of the track by team and sleighs and marching 23 miles further on; on flat cars, uncovered and open with the thermometer at 50 degrees below. Huron Bay, Jackfish, McKay's Harbour were passed by alternate flat cars on construction tracks; and, teaming in fearful weather round the north shore of Lake Superior, Nipigon was reached... the men had no sleep for four nights."

The first group under Gen. F.D. Middleton encountered the Métis on April 24 with half his original force. After a short battle Middleton decided to wait until his forces reunited before pushing on. Aware of Middleton's predicament Riel tried to mount a united attack of his own but his suspicious Indians were too slow off the mark.

Lieut.-Col. W.D. Otter, commanding the second force, relieved Battleford and marched on to find Chief Poundmaker's Indians still on their reserve. Otter attacked on May 2, hoping to surprise the Indians. He failed and retreated to high ground. After a day of fighting Otter withdrew to Battleford under cover of his Gatling gun. Poundmaker and a number of Cree warriors moved toward Batoche, Riel's headquarters. On May 14 they intercepted a supply train and took a number of prisoners.

Meanwhile, Gen. Middleton, after spending two weeks at Fish Creek, moved against Batoche. After a

PAC PA25531

Maj.-Gen. Frederick D. Middleton (1825-1898) in 1884. After a notable career in various parts of the Empire, he was appointed commander of the Canadian Militia in 1884. He was knighted after his success in suppressing the Northwest Rebellion.

week of fighting Riel surrendered. Middleton then moved to defeat Poundmaker. The Rebellion collapsed.

On November 7, 1885, Donald Smith hammered in the last spike on the Canadian Pacific Railway connecting the east and west coasts. In the event of further civil unrest the army now had the ability to move swiftly to any point across the nation and meet the threat.

(Overleaf)
North-West Mounted Police barracks and square, Regina, N.W.T., 1885. The NWMP was established along military lines in 1873 to maintain law and order in the Northwest Territories. It became the Royal North-West Mounted Police in 1904 and the RCMP in 1919.

PAC PA118756

PAC C17630A

(Above) Militia at Winnipeg on the way to the Northwest Rebellion, and (below) coulee at Fort Qu'Appelle, N.W.T. The 12th and 35th regiments and the Winnipeg Cavalry are shown passing through the Touchwood Hills to Humboldt. Lieut.-Col William E. O'Brien, on the white horse, commanded the York and Simcoe battalions.

PAC C1876

Ontario Archives

(Left) Members of the Governor General's Body-guard at Wells Hill Camp during the Northwest Rebellion.

(Overleaf) Edgar Dewdney, lieutenant governor of the Northwest Territories, meeting the Indian chief Pie-a-Pot and braves, 1885.

PAC PA118775

(Below) "Prairie Church Parade of General Middleton's Command."

Royal Ontario Museum, Toronto

PAC C5824

(Above) Train at a prairie depot during the Northwest Rebellion, 1885.

(Right) A studio photograph of Lieut. Arthur Howard behind a Gatling gun used in the Northwest Rebellion.

(Facing page)
(Above) Officers of the Governor General's Bodyguard, Humboldt, N.W.T., 1885. (Below) Asleep in the trenches.

PAC C1882

(Above) The Battle of Fish Creek. The rebels' rifle fire can be seen in the woods across the creek at the lower right. Gen. Middleton watches the progress of the battle from horse-back at the centre left of the litho-graph.

(Right) Sewing corpses into canvas in preparation for burial, Fish Creek. This photo and the one that follows were taken by Capt. James Peters.

Gun pit, "A" Battery, Regiment of Canadian Artillery, at
Fish Creek, April 24, 1885.

Gen. Middleton with his wounded aides.

(Overleaf)
The capture of Batoche. The lithograph
includes the following key: 1 Trail to Carlton
($10\frac{1}{2}$ miles). 2 South branch of River
Saskatchewan. 3 Batoche's Ferry (Fisher's
Crossing). 4 Trail to Humboldt ($63\frac{1}{2}$ miles).
5 Half-breed camp. 6 Batoche's House.
7 House whence loyal prisoners were
liberated. 8 Fifth line of rifle pits. 9 Ploughed
land, where our men suffered most.
10 Fourth line of rifle pits. 11 Third line of
rifle pits. 12 Second line of rifle pits. 13 First
line of defences. 14,15 Redels firing from
west bank. 16 Midland Battalion clearing
rifle pits along river bank. 17 Midland
Battalion. 18,19,20,21 Royal Grenadiers.
22,23 90th Batt. Rifles. 24 Boulton's
Mounted Infantry and French's Scouts.
25 9-pounder M.L.R. gun (Winnipeg Field
Battery). 26 Grenadiers Ambulance Corps.
27 "The Man with the Gatling."
28 9-pounder M.L.R. gun ("A" Battery).

Royal Ontario Museum, Toronto

PAC C3463

(Above) Shelling Batoche, the last shot before the attack on the guns.

(Right) The Indian Miserable Man surrendering at Battleford, 1885.

PAC C17374

74

Riel, a prisoner, in another photo by Capt. James Peters.

General Lord A.G. Russell and his staff. He became the British commander of forces in Nova Scotia, including the garrison.

ON FOREIGN SERVICE

In England, Gen. Lord Wolseley was placed in command of a relief force for Gen. Gordon under siege at Khartoum. Drawing on his Canadian experiences, Wolseley suggested taking some Canadian voyageurs as boatmen to negotiate the Nile. However, with the completion of the railroad the voyageurs had ceased to exist. Instead, in 1884 a force of 386 lumbermen and Indians was raised for service with the Nile Expedition. Wolseley's force reached Khartoum too late to save Gordon. Although the Canadians' term of service was for only six months, nearly a third of the force remained in Egypt for over a year.

At the same time a variety of rebellious incidents about the Empire prompted Britain to suggest that Canada might—as had New South Wales (later Australia in 1900)—make troops available for service with the British Army. Canadian newspapers and Prime Minister Macdonald were vigorously opposed to the idea.

Gold was discovered in the Yukon in 1896 and tens of thousands of fortune-seekers flocked into the territory. Fears in Ottawa that an American takeover of the Yukon might be in the offing led to the formation of the Yukon Field Force to bolster the few NWMP officers headquartered at Dawson. In May 1898 a force of 203 volunteers commanded by Lieut.-Col. T.D.B. Evans set out by train from Ottawa to save the Yukon from annexation by the U.S.

The force diarist wrote: "Arrived in Winnipeg after two days and nights of boredom marched off through cheering crowds where a citizens welcoming committee had laid on a wagon load of beer for the troops. Lots of speeches and silliness. At last, filled with beer and good wishes everybody staggered back to the train accompanied by the band of the 90th Regiment playing The Maple Leaf Forever."

Embarrassingly, access to the Yukon lay through American lands and waters. However, once the men, arms and equipment were aboard "in bond" at Vancouver, the U.S. customs inspection in Alaskan coastal waters became little more than a formality and they waved the force on to Fort Wrangel, a coastal port on the Alaskan Panhandle.

"Troops from the local U.S. Army detachment—mostly coloured—gave us a friendly welcome," the diarist observed. "Hard to believe that these are the same enemy forces plotting to take over the Yukon. I wonder if it isn't all just a case of somebody in Ottawa crying Wolf! Wolf!"

The force moved by boat up the Stikine River to Glenora then on to Telegraph Creek and from there by mule train to Teslin Lake. From Teslin the route switched overland through swamps, fallen trees, cutting rocks, clouds of insects and alternate heavy rains and blazing sun. The men drilled continuously among the rocks and stumps to maintain their military bearing. They reached Fort Selkirk on September 11. An initial detachment of 52 men reached the goldfields on October 1, 1898, to become the first Canadian troops to serve above the Arctic Circle.

The following year the start of the Boer War raised the question of Imperial defence once again. This time the Canadian public was behind the idea of supporting Britain. Prime Minister Sir Wilfrid Laurier agreed reluctantly to send troops. In all, Canada provided 7368 officers and men for service in South Africa. The Canadian government absorbed the cost for training and travel and made up the difference between the British and Canadian pay rates while the

Militia NCOs at Camp Niagara, 1888.

Capt. T.D.B. Evans, Winnipeg, 1892. He was later Lieut.-Col. in charge of the Yukon Field Force that went north at the time of the gold rush. Note the arms collection on the wall. Evans was an avid weapons collector.

Militia parade down Brock Street, Kingston, 1889.

troops were stationed in Africa. The total cost came to under $3 million, an enormous sum for the time in a country with a shade over 5 million population and no income tax.

The men of the Royal Canadian Dragoons marched 1700 miles and took part in 79 engagements. Troops of the 2nd Canadian Mounted Rifles marched 2600 miles and took part in 15 separate engagements and a half dozen skirmishes. In one stand near Honing Spruit four men of the 2nd C.M.R. courageously held off 50 Boers. Two of them died, two were wounded. In action at Lelifontein a handful of dismounted Canadians held off an attack by 200 Boers, who charged to within 70 yards of the line. As a result of this action three Canadians received Victoria Crosses. All had been militiamen. One of them, Lieut. R.E.W. Turner, went on to become Lieut.-Gen. Sir Richard Turner, commander of a Canadian division during World War I.

Back in Canada the South African War divided the French and English. Quebec was not prepared to support any war on behalf of England. Protests erupted all over the province and only Laurier's tremendous personal popularity managed to keep the opposition in check. In English Canada the war strengthened Imperial ties while at the same time establishing the nation's position as an independent country capable of deciding for itself whether or not to go to war.

A New Army

By 1899 the Canadian militia had been transformed into a self-contained citizen army organized into brigades and divisions under specially selected commanders who were assisted by adequate staff. At the same time a start was made on organizing various service units. The Royal Canadian Engineers was established in 1903; a Canadian Army Medical Corps came into existence the following year.

The new Canadian Ross rifle became the weapon of the militia. Canada's permanent force was increased to 2000. All criticism of military expense ceased abruptly when the militia was used to put down labour troubles in Sydney Mines, Kingston, Hamilton and Winnipeg in the period between 1905 and 1909. The tradition of using British-trained officers to command militia units was terminated after a series of opinionated Englishmen had made

themselves thoroughly unpopular with both the government and the army. Thereafter, commanders were answerable to a Militia Council consisting of the minister of national defence, his deputy minister, the department's accountant and the four heads of the staff branches.

The threat of Germany and the triple alliance caused Britain to pull its garrison out of Halifax. Canada was left to defend her own territorial waters. The Permanent Force was hastily increased to 4000 and the elaborate Halifax dockyard complex became Canadian government property. In the years leading up to the First World War, England attempted to make Imperial solidarity the new aim for its defence policy. At the Imperial Defence Conference held in London in 1909, agreement was reached for harmonizing the military forces of Britain and the colonies in such a way that in an emergency they could easily be combined into a single fighting force. This meant that training, whether in London, Ottawa or Melbourne, would be identical. Although the concept made for an extremely organized fighting force, Canadians lost their independence and uniqueness. Canadian abilities for river, mountain and forest terrain and acclimatization for cold weather combat were ignored by the British.

"C" Battery, Royal Canadian Artillery, camped at Skeena
River, B.C., 1888.

St. Catharines Ladies School Cadet Corps, 1891,
developed during the enthusiastic period of the women's
suffrage movement to prove that "the female of the species
was more deadly than the male...."

(Facing page)
(Above) Officers of the 16th Battalion, Brockville Militia,
1893. (Below) Camp Kingston, near the Royal Military
College, 1896.

1893

Ontario Archives

PAC C1330

84

(Facing page)
(Above) Officers' tent mess during militia training, Peta-wawa, 1897. White linen, silverware and monogrammed English bone china were considered necessities of daily mess life regardless of living conditions. (Below) The Yukon Field Force at Fort Selkirk, Yukon.

The Yukon Field Force changing the guard at the NWMP barracks, Dawson, Yukon, 1899. The force withdrew the following year.

Field Marshal Viscount Wolseley in 1900. Garnet Wolseley (1833-1913), like Gen. Middleton and many other career officers in the British army, was Irish-born. He first came to Canada in 1861 after service in India, the Crimea and China and ended his career as commander in chief of the British army.

Maj.-Gen. O'Grady Haly, commander of Canadian forces, 1900-1902.

Members of Lord Strathcona's Horse aboard SS *Monterey*. CPR backer Lord Strathcona, who was high commissioner in London at the time, raised and financed this regiment of over 500 mounted riflemen during the South African War.

PAC PA113042

PAC PA113025

(Facing page)
(Above) Personnel of the 2nd Canadian Mounted Rifles in camp at Newcastle, Natal, 1902, and (below) a supply convoy preparing to depart in Natal, 1902.

(Right) Boer Gen. De la Rey coming in to negotiate the surrender of the last Boer commando.

(Below) Personnel of the 2nd Canadian Mounted Rifles en route from Volksrust to Klerksdorp, Transvaal, March 1902.

PAC C22275

PAC PA113029

Durban Camp, South Africa, June 1902.

PAC PA34097

Ottawa—return of soldiers from the South African War.

(Overleaf) Warrant officers, staff sergeants and sergeants,
Royal Canadian Garrison Artillery, Quebec, 1903.

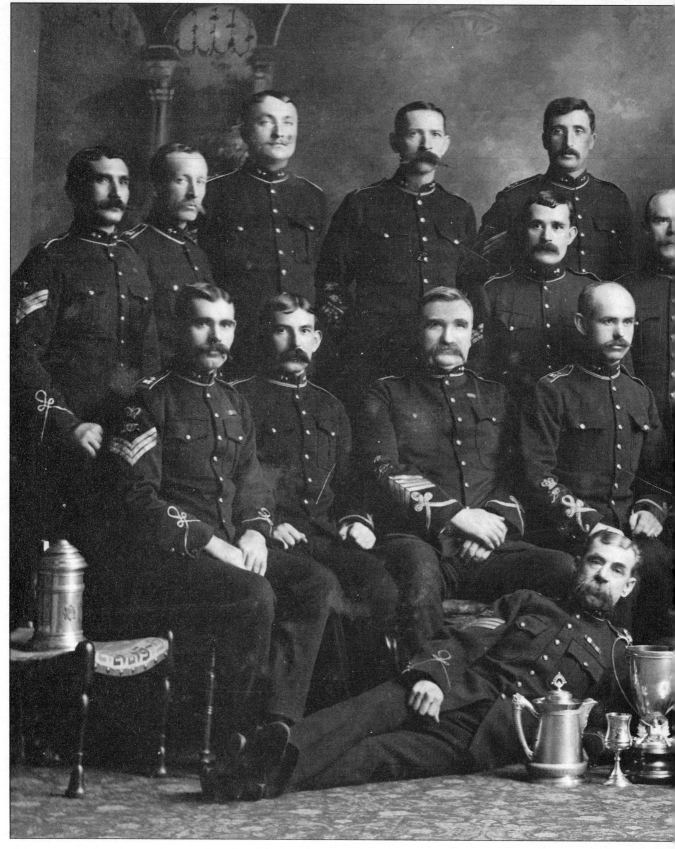

Marchpast of the Queen's Own Rifles at Camp Aldershot, England, in 1910. Sir Henry Pellatt brought the group from Canada at his own expense.

(Facing page)
(Above) Band of the 2nd Dragoons Militia at Camp Petawawa, 1912, and (below) militia volunteers from Carleton county at Petawawa in 1910.

(Facing page)
(Above) Mounting an 18-pounder quick-firing gun on a farmer's sleigh, and (below) militiamen struggling with a frozen-in gun during exercises at Verona, Ont., February 1910. Weekend exercises of this sort went on all year with every militia unit.

(Left) The entrance to the Citadel, Halifax, 1902.

(Below) The 31st Regiment at Camp Niagara, June 1906.

HUNG. 2066 NIAGARA CAMP. 31ST REGT AT MCRE 23 JUNE 1906

A.deL. Panet Collection/PAC PA117578

A.deL. Panet Collection/PAC PA117576

A sea of canvas was the first sight that greeted recruits at the vast camps that were training and staging centres for Canada's newly expanded army. Shown here is Valcartier, near Quebec.

WORLD WAR I

The Great War began at midnight, Tuesday, August 4, 1914. King George V of England was in the fourth year of his reign. The British Empire was at the summit of its power and global influence. During the four years it ran, the war developed into a conflict pitting Germany, the Austrian Empire and Turkey against everyone else. Prime Minister Sir Robert Borden had wired London three days before hostilities began offering Canada's support with 22,000 troops and a pledge to raise a half million men by 1916, an ambitious undertaking for a nation with a population of not quite 8 million.

Valcartier, a sandy plain 16 miles northwest of Quebec City, was chosen for the assembly area. By early September 33,000 men and 7000 horses had arrived from militia units across the country. The force sailed on October 3 in 32 ships. Once ashore in England the Canadians were established on the bleak Salisbury Plain. The plain's thin clay soil covered an underlying base of limestone that prevented any rain runoff. The fall and winter turned out to be the wettest in 60 years. In one three-month period only five days were without rain. One of the Canadian medical officers wrote: "Our men are now crowded into makeshift wood frame and canvas covered huts which are better than living in the mud under tents.... Everybody is still damp, bored and homesick. Influenza, subacute enteritis and meningitis have broken out. For the first time I understand how England built her empire. It was done by men desperate to escape the English climate at any price!"

The British War Office was under the impression that the Canadians were fully equipped and ready for action. Nothing could have been further from the truth. One inspection on the Salisbury Plain and any thought of sending the men to France in December was abandoned. The Ross rifle turned out to be useless in mud, Canadian cardboard boots fell apart in the rain, the turning radius of horsedrawn wagons was too large for English and European roads. Close to $5 million worth of supplies and materials purchased in Canada had to be abandoned in favour of standard British army issue for everything from boots and blankets to vehicles and horse harness. It was an embarrassing beginning to the country's participation in the Great War.

By late November, while the Canadians sat soaking at Salisbury Plain, the war across the Channel had changed from the fluid movement of men, guns and horses to a series of trenches, barbed wire and shell holes stretching from the Belgian coast to the Swiss border 300 miles to the southeast. Over the next four years, as the vast opposing armies tried wearing each other down, changes along the lines could be measured in yards.

The Canadians arrived at the front on March 3, 1915. A few days later men of the Princess Patricia's Canadian Light Infantry stopped a fierce counterattack near the French town of Ypres. The British generals conducting the campaign were satisfied with the performance. One wrote his corps commander: "Our Canadian troops have been blooded nicely and their line has held."

Any lingering doubts the British generals might have had about the quality of Canadian troops was dispelled a month later when on April 22 the Germans launched their first gas attack of the war. Troops manning the second line of trenches watched in bewilderment as British, French and Canadians came running towards them in panic and confusion, staggering over the parapets to collapse in the agonies of suffocation. Some urinated in their socks and undershirts and wrapped them around their faces to keep out the fumes. Others tried holding their breath until the main cloud has passed. Behind the cloud of creeping gas and wearing new protective gas masks came the German infantry. Some of the fiercest fighting of the war took place in the days that followed. By next afternoon the Germans had pushed the French and British back until the Canadian troops were fighting on three fronts. Nevertheless, they held their positions until relieved by British forces on April 29. Three thousand men were listed

Camp Borden, near Barrie, Ont., was named after Sir Frederick Borden, who was minister of militia and defence, 1896-1911, and was responsible for reforming and modernizing the Canadian militia.

as killed, wounded or missing.

Month after month the war swayed on as the bravest of a generation perished in the senseless slaughter. Gallipoli, a fiasco in the Turkish Dardenelles, became the Ypres for Australian, New Zealand and British troops, who took 100,000 casualties before being withdrawn. Nearly 700,000 French and German soldiers were lost at the battles of Verdun. Seven entire villages disappeared. Along a 25-mile battlefield on the Somme the British army lost 60,000 men in one day, 500,000 in five months. At Lys, Passchendaele—one place after another—generals gambled away their armies. After the Nivelles offensive in April 1917, the French army mutinied. Five miles northeast of Arras, Canadian forces stormed and captured Vimy Ridge, an astonishing feat of arms that neither the French nor the British had been able to manage during three years of repeated attacks. The Canadian army overseas

grew to six divisions under the leadership of Lieut.-Gen. Arthur Currie, "the best general of the lot!" according to British Prime Minister David Lloyd George, who considered giving Currie overall command of British forces on the Western Front if the war lasted.

The dying, wounded, maimed and blinded poured back across the Channel to England. For the first time since the Napoleonic Wars each nation's army found itself starved for reserves to replace the appalling front line losses. Although Germany and Britain relied on conscripts to fill the ranks, Canada remained steadfast in its concept of a volunteer citizen army. But by the summer of 1917 the problem of replacements was causing serious political discord at home. The problem was perceived by troops at the front to be French Quebec. Of the 300,000 Canadian soldiers overseas in 1917 fewer than 15,000 were French Canadian. It was an issue that threatened to tear the country apart. The fault lay not so much with French Canada's distaste for a European war as with the bigotry of English Canada's defence establishment that flatly refused to permit the Quebecois to serve together in their own linguistic regimental or battalion groups. In the end the Germans solved the Allied problem of replacements by infuriating the Americans to the point where they entered the war. By midsummer of 1917 the United States had 1.5 million men in training camps across the country and by the following summer 300,000 American troops a month were crossing the Atlantic. The advantage shifted quickly to the Allied side. The stalemate of trench warfare ended. Germany was finished.

The formalities concluded with an Armistice on November 11, 1918. German honour was salvaged from the humiliation of defeat. The troops sailed home while well meaning but naive politicians laid the groundwork for another world war two decades later.

Between the Wars

The League of Nations came into being on January 1, 1920. It was, according to its charter, designed "to prevent future wars by establishing relations on the basis of justice and honour and to promote co-operation, material and intellectual, between the nations of the world." There were to be no more

Col. Sam Hughes (centre) and an unidentified lieutenant-colonel at Valcartier, 1914. More energetic than skilful, the colourful Sam Hughes (1853-1921) was fired from his cabinet position in charge of the militia by Prime Minister Borden in 1916. Hughes holds the distinction of being the only serving officer to apply personally for a Victoria Cross (it was refused).

PAC PA4964

An army motor car is rescued by horses at Larkhill, Salisbury Plain, England. Mud was the chief memory of those who passed through the Salisbury Plain camps.

wars. Twenty-eight allied and 14 neutral states, including Canada, jumped on board this improbable bandwagon. The United States restrained its earlier enthusiasm and abstained. Membership later increased to 60 states, each promising never to go to war with a fellow state until all possibilities of a peaceful settlement had been exhausted, and then only after an interval of nine months.

In this euphoria of post-war resolve, Canada's permanent force shrank to 4000. The only real excitement for the small peace-time army came during a spate of union unrest and civil disobedience in Cape Breton, Toronto and Winnipeg. Permanent force detachments were called out to prevent bloodshed and restore law and order. In each distasteful situation the troops acquitted themselves with good humour and restraint. Yet despite the need for a military presence from time to time, successive government austerity programs left the army with little in the way of political support, new equipment or new thinking.

Interest in the militia waned also. By 1930 it had been reduced to little more than a social grazing ground for ex-soldiers and young enthusiastic recruits who enjoyed the annual three weeks of soldiering and camaraderie at the summer training camps across the country. Thought of another war became the furthest thing from anyone's mind. Troop training programs remained identical to those of 1918. Cavalry, already outdated by the machine gun and tank, was still considered the best method for rapid reconnaissance in the field and a mobile force to be reckoned with. When imaginative junior officers and NCOs pointed out the dangers of such assumptions, they were either ignored or sternly rebuked for overstepping their authority.

A few, like E.L.M Burns, Churchill Mann and F.F.

Worthington—all of whom would later become generals—refused to be intimidated. Through their efforts and a few others like them, common sense prevailed and the Canadian Army began cautiously to experiment with mobile armour— tanks, armoured cars, self-propelled guns and armoured carriers. It wasn't much but it was a start.

Meanwhile, the high-minded ideals of the Geneva-based League of Nations dissolved into a morass of indecision over the refusal of some of its member nations to abide by the solemn promises they had given earlier to the world body. It was a decade of European dictatorships, Benito Mussolini in Italy, Adolf Hitler in Germany and Francisco Franco in Spain. Each had his vision of public adoration and national pride. For Mussolini it was to recapture the glory of Rome by invading the black Kingdom of Ethiopia. Bombers and guns against spears and bows and arrows. The outcome was never in doubt.

Hitler viewed himself as a patriot and the saviour of German honour after the country's economic

A 6-inch breech-loading gun at Ives Point Battery, McNab Island, Halifax, 1915. The battery guarded the approach to Halifax Harbour. The battery was one of seven interlocking fields of fire covering the approaches.

collapse, territorial dismemberment and crushing reparations imposed by the Allied powers after the war. Franco's dream was to lead the overthrow of a corrupt monarchy and prevent a communist takeover. With Hitler's help he succeeded. Germany and Japan withdrew from the League of Nations in 1935, Italy in 1937. As Hitler rearmed his nation, successfully bluffing and threatening his way into the Rhineland, Austria and Czechoslovakia, the terrible realization began to dawn on the governments of France, England and the dominions that there was only one way to halt the threat of a Europe dominated by Hitler and Mussolini. For the second time within a single generation the world went back to war.

Ontario Archives

Halifax Citadel Collection

PAC C30372

Barbed wire on the Western Front, and (right) a
camouflaged observation post.

PAC 30373

(Facing page)
The Prince of Wales inspects troops at the CNE grounds,
Toronto, 1915, and (below) King George V at a graduation
ceremony of the Royal Flying Corps, 1915.

PAC PA16

PAC C30356

PAC PA636

(Facing page)
Repair car, equipped with lathe and other tools, June 1916. This mobile machine shop was the forerunner of the REME. (Below) A damaged armoured car.

(Above) A horse-drawn ambulance, September 1916.
(Below) A line of lorries waiting to take ammunition to the front. Dangerous work performed only at night to avoid shelling and stray bombs.

PAC PA12

PAC PA742

A shell-burst in a trench wounds a member of the 5th Battalion. Trenches were invariably ankle-deep in mud.

Salvaging equipment on the battlefield, July 1916.

O.28

Kite balloons were used for aerial observation of enemy positions. This sequence of photos shows a kite balloon being readied for an ascent, the pilot and observer in the basket, and the balloon aloft. No parachutes were worn. If an enemy aircraft appeared, the ground crew worked frantically to winch the balloon and basket down before the hydrogen-filled bag ignited from an incendiary bullet and the crew crashed to earth.

Testing a Vickers machine gun, September 1916. The water-cooled Vickers became the workhorse of the infantry in trench warfare.

(Facing page)
Loading ammunition on a light railway, September 1916, and (below) 15-inch shells, presents from Canada to Germany.

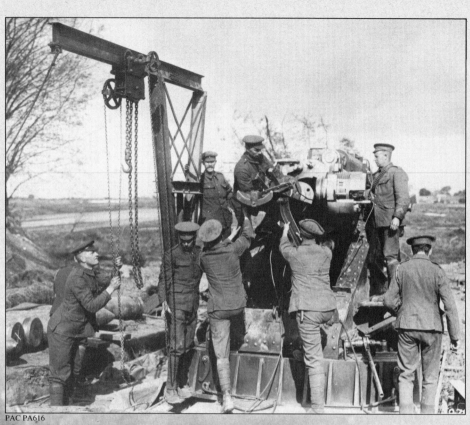

Loading a heavy howitzer,
September 1916, and
(below) a heavy howitzer
in action.

(Above) Moving heavy guns up to new positions, October 1916. Notice the clumps of mud on everyone's boots. This road is relatively dry! (Below) Canadian troops in a communication trench, September 1916.

(Facing page)
Air photo of Stuff Redoubt by No.7 Squadron, Royal Flying Corps, September 1916.

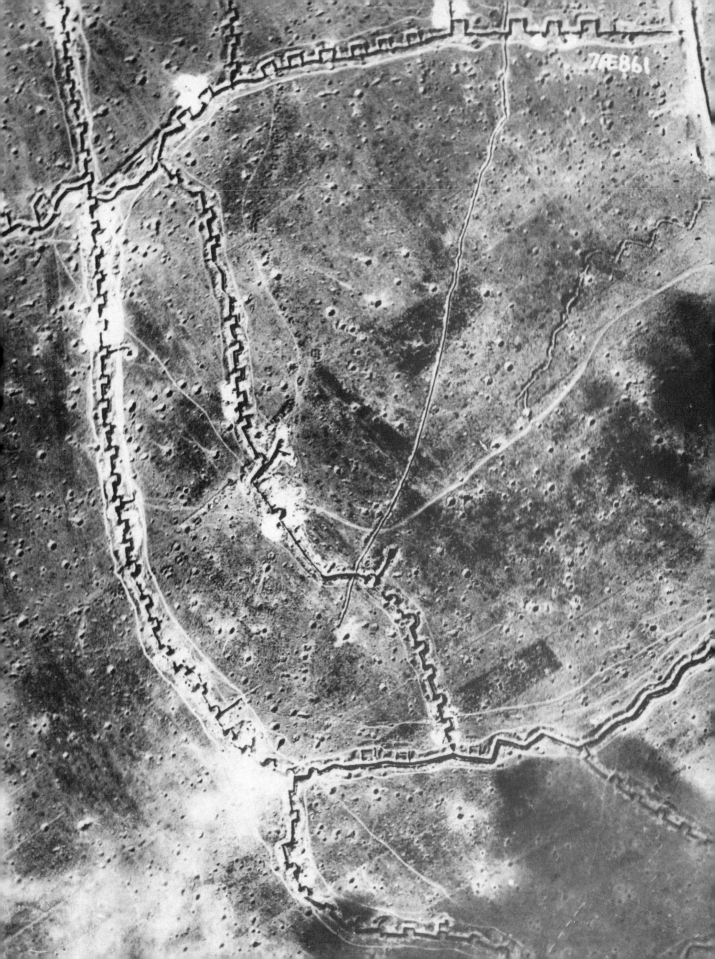

Halifax Citadel Collection

PAC PA743

118

PAC PA568

(Facing page)
(Above) A historic photo taken at Thieval, September 15, 1916, during the Battle of the Somme, showing tanks in action for the first time. Forty-nine were used with great success in this engagement by British forces, and (below) swabbing out the barrel of a howitzer after a barrage. Note steam rising from the breech as the gunner withdraws the water-soaked swab.

On sentry duty in the front-line trench, September 1916.

Canadian hospital ward, France, 1916. Canadian medical services were acknowledged as the best at the front and behind the lines.

Ontario Archives

A few of the empties fired in the Canadians' attack on Vimy Ridge, May 1917.

Lieut.-Gen. Sir Julian Byng, seen here with some of his personal staff in May 1917, was appointed to command the Canadian Corps in 1916. He led it in the attack on Vimy Ridge and was subsequently made commander of the British Third Army. Viscount Byng of Vimy (1862-1935) was appointed governor general of Canada in 1921.

Gen. Currie, commander of the Canadian troops in France, June 1917. Sir Arthur Currie (1875-1933) was born in Strathroy, Ont., and although he entered the war with no military experience besides militia duty, he rose to become commander of the Canadian Corps by June 1917. Regarded as a first-rate field commander, he turned his talents after the war to university administration as principal and vice-chancellor of McGill, where he was an equal success.

Tanks waiting to go into action, July 1917.

A Canadian narrow-gauge armoured train taking ammunition up to the line through a badly shelled village. The railways ran as far back as 20 miles from the front.
PAC PA1757

PAC PA4330

Building dummy tanks on the Somme, 1916. There were few real tanks available. Wooden dummies gave German aircraft and balloon observers food for thought.

PAC PA1466

Canadians being issued with summer underwear in reserve trenches, June 1917.

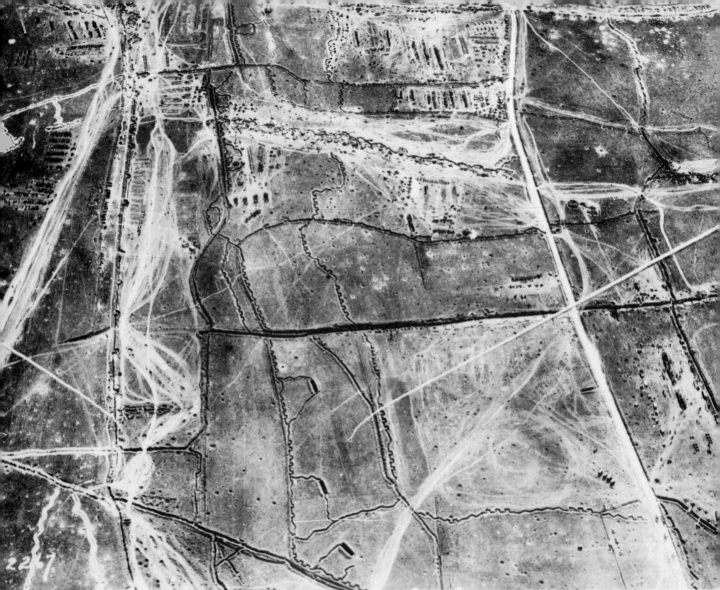

Trenches on Vimy Ridge, photographed from a kite balloon, November 1917.

(Facing page)
Horses going through a bath (above) containing chemicals to prevent disease, September 1917. (Below) Tanks advancing down the Amiens-Roye road, Battle of Amiens, August 1917.

PAC PA3713

PAC PA3127

126

Brig.-Gen. A.G.L. McNaughton with Gen. Currie, 1918. Andrew McNaughton (1887-1966) ended the war as commander of the Canadian Corps artillery. Between the wars he rose to become chief of the general staff.

PAC C18120

Antony d'Ypres

Memorial to the Unkown Soldiers of the British armies, Ypres.

Antony d'Ypres

Memorial to the 85th Canadian Battalion (Nova Scotia Highlanders), Passchendaele.

(Facing page)
(Above) Lieut.-Col. Moshier, Capt. Grant and Capt. Turnbull, 11th Field Ambulance, outside captured German dug-out, August 1918. (Below) Canadians and prisoners take cover in a trench during the advance east of Arras, September 1918. At this point in the war neither side was interested in heroics. Note the embarrassed smiles of relief on the German faces.

Personnel of the Lake Superior Regiment learning to fire a
2-inch mortar at Aldershot in 1942. Left to right, Privates
S. Folster and D. Blellock and Sgt. B.W. Wright.

WORLD WAR II

The Second World War began at midnight, September 1, 1939, when the Germany Army marched into Poland. Two days later, England and France, which had guaranteed Polish independence, declared war. Within the week Britain's dominions followed suit. The Canadian Department of National Defence authorized creation of the Canadian Active Service Force (CASF) to be composed of two divisions. Enlistment was voluntary with most men entering directly from the Active Militia. Maj.-Gen. A.G.L. McNaughton , former Chief of the General Staff, became "Inspector General of the Units of the 1st Canadian Division."

The flurry of new appointments, promotions and righteous speeches by the sanctimonious politicians of the Mackenzie King government did little to mask the nation's dreadful state of preparedness. What arms were available were nearly all of 1914-18 vintage. Mobile transport was virtually non-existent. and there were only 16 light tanks in the entire country. A Permanent Force captain recently returned from Staff College in England, who later became a major-general, wrote in October 1939: "...the fine spirit of Canada in this party is inspired by selfish motives. Politicians make pretty speeches about the wonderful aid we are giving being paid for by the British taxpayer. They are to make Canada the training centre for the Empire air forces. Secretly everyone rejoices because they see financial benefits. Meanwhile thousands of splendid fellows drill furiously in poor clothing having given up good jobs to kill Germans. It's going to be mighty interesting to see how it all works out. The men of the CASF are wonderful material. Wish I could say the same for our politicians."

The 1st Division, consisting of three brigades, sailed from Halifax in convoy during December. The idea of sending the men directly to France in support of British troops who were backing the French army was quickly quashed in favour of giving the Canadians a period of training in England. A German invasion of France and the Low Countries was not anticipated before spring. Instead of the Salisbury Plain, the men were billeted at Camp Aldershot. Conditions were primitive and overcrowded— 1500-man units crammed into badly heated barracks designed for 850. Bad food and churlish British junior officers added to their discomfort. Throughout the winter the men trained and sat waiting.

This *Sitzkreig* or phony war ended on May 10, 1940, when German troops crossed the border into Holland and Belgium. To a scramble of countermanding orders, Canadian troops moved to Scotland to embark for Norway. When that was cancelled they returned to Aldershot; then after several more weeks of on-again-off-again alerts the 1st Brigade sailed for Brest under Brig. Armand Smith to aid in the evacuation of British and French troops. No sooner had the men landed and boarded their train than the French army capitulated. After a frantic ride into Rennes, Smith ordered the engineer to make for St. Malo, where, after leaving most of their heavy equipment behind, the force embarked on one of the last British vessels leaving the continent. The men returned to Aldershot and settled down to training .

Germany invaded Greece and the Balkans. Gen. Erwin Rommel captured most of North Africa from the British. Hong Kong and Singapore fell to Hitler's Japanese allies. A small Canadian force sent to bolster British defences at Hong Kong was taken

The West Nova Scotia Regiment on parade at Aldershot
and on the march, 1940.

Both: Halifax Citadel Army Museum

prisoner a few weeks after its arrival. The Germans invaded Russia and reached the gates of Moscow. Meanwhile, back in England, the Canadians continued their training. The monotony was interrupted twice, the first time briefly in August 1941, when Brig. Arthur Potts led a small Canadian raiding force of 527 men to the archipelago of Spitzbergen, Norway, 600 miles north of the Arctic Circle. The force sailed on the *Empress of Canada* accompanied by two cruisers and three destroyers. Its task was to destroy Spitzbergen's coal reserves and remove 2000 Russian inhabitants to the Russian port of Archangel. The force completed the operation and arrived safely back in England during early September.

The second training interruption took place a year later with tragic results. On the night of August 18, 1942, a force of 5000 Canadians, 1057 British commando troops and a detachment of American Rangers carried out a raid against the French coastal resort town of Dieppe. Its purpose was to get information about German defences and learn what could be expected during a large-scale assault on a strongly defended Channel port. The element of surprise was lost during the approach to the French coast when the British naval flotilla came under fire from enemy trawlers which were quickly reinforced with other German ships.

Several ships disembarked troops after dawn 30 minutes late and at once came under heavy fire. Because the anti-tank defences had not been destroyed by naval and air bombardment, the 28 tanks that were landed could not give adequate support and had to be abandoned. While the principal objective of the air operations was to support the landing parties, a great air battle developed in which 48 German aircraft were destroyed against 106 losses by the RAF and RCAF. Casualties were heavy; 3372 Canadians were killed, wounded or captured. British forces lost a further 1000 men. German losses amounted to 600. The valuable lessons learned from the Dieppe disaster were put to good use in planning for the invasion of Normandy.

Throughout the remaining months of 1942 and into early 1943, while the men trained on every conceivable tactical condition and situation, political pressure began building in Canada for its troops to get into the war. The British, the Free French, the Czechs and Poles in exile, even the Americans who

PAC C18246

Gen. McNaughton with Prime Minister W.L. Mackenzie King at Aldershot in August 1941. McNaughton was in charge of Canada's army in the U.K. and fought hard to keep Canadian forces together as a unit. He resigned his command in 1943 and served briefly as minister of national defence but his political career fell victim to the conscription crisis.

had entered the war in December 1941, were fighting the common enemy while Canadian soldiers continued to train in England. It was becoming an embarrassment.

In London, during the last week of April 1943, Gen. Sir Alan Brooke, Chief of the Imperial Defence Staff, invited Lieut.-Gen. McNaughton to the War Office for a chat. McNaughton was told that as a result of the Casablanca conference three months earlier between British Prime Minister Churchill, Russia's dictator Stalin and U.S. President Roosevelt, a decision had been made to attack Germany through its "soft underbelly," as Churchill had put it. McNaughton was asked if Canada would be interested in participating in such an operation in the Mediterranean by supplying one infantry division and a tank brigade together with necessary support troops. There was one hitch: the force would be operating exclusively under British control and command. Within 48 hours Ottawa had given its blessings to the project. Eleven weeks later Canadian troops were landing on the beaches of Sicily.

Simultaneously, Canada received an invitation from Washington to participate in retaking the American Aleutian island of Kiska. During May, in one of the bloodiest assaults of the war up until that time, American troops had recaptured the Aleutian island of Attu. Although the American force outnumbered them 10 to 1 it took two weeks to subdue the 2500 fanatical Japanese defenders. Thirty prisoners were taken. The rest were either killed or committed suicide. Only Kiska remained in Japanese hands.

The Canadian War Cabinet approved the use of a domestically based Canadian brigade group numbering 5300. Brig. Harry Foster was brought back from England to command it. The 35,000 Canadian and American troops sailed in convoy from the Aleutian island of Adak on August 13, a Friday, and arrived off Kiska two days later. The assault turned out to be an embarrassing fiasco when it was discovered that the Japanese had evacuated the island two weeks earlier.

Sicily turned out to be quite a different sort of party. With 3000 ships, the combined force of the American Seventh Army and British Eighth Army to which the Canadians were attached, arrived off the southern part of the island on July 10 and stormed ashore at various landing points. The landings resulted in the collapse of the Italian government, with Mussolini placed under arrest. It took 38 days to capture Sicily. German and Italian casualties amounted to 165,000 against 25,000 among the British, American and Canadians. On September 3 the Eighth Army crossed the 3.5 miles over the Straits of Messina to the mainland and began a methodical advance up the Italian peninsula. Two days later the new head of the Italian government, Marshal Badoglio, signed a secret armistice with the Allies. Most of the Italian battle fleet escaped to the British held island of Malta and the port of Alexandria in Egypt.

An airborne descent to capture the airfields around Rome had to be aborted when the Germans seized them. As a result the Allies were unable to secure fighter protection for landings any farther north than Salerno. There on September 9 the Fifth Army—a mix of British and Americans—under command of U.S. Gen. Mark Clark came ashore. The landing permitted the Allied advance north to continue. The Germans fell back slowly, finally stabilizing their front across a narrow part of the peninsula on the Ortona-Garigliano line. Thereafter operations were held up by torrential seasonal rains and both sides hunkered down for the winter.

The stalemate was broken on January 22, 1944, when Canadian, American and British troops landed behind the German lines south of Rome at the Anzio-Nettuno beachhead. The Germans fought back stubbornly, containing the Anzio pocket. Four months passed before the men from the beachhead were joined by the main Allied army in an offensive that opened on May 12 and carried the Allied armies into Rome and beyond.

The Italian campaign became the training ground for many of Canada's combat leaders who were later assigned to the Normandy invasion. Generals. Crerar, Simonds, Vokes, Kitching, Jefferson and a host of others owed their "blooding" for command to the time spent serving in the "Spaghetti League." From a single infantry division in British Gen. Sir Oliver Leese's XXX Corps in the Eighth Army during the invasion of Sicily, Canadian forces had grown into a corps of two divisions (1st Infantry and 5th Armoured) and an armoured brigade. In March 1944, when Lieut.-Gen. Harry Crerar was appointed Canadian Army Commander, he turned over 76,000

Nicholas Morant/PAC PA137850

Shells for 9.2-inch coastal defence gun, probably at Alert Head, British Columbia, 1941.

"*Come on Pal*... YOU'RE NEEDED UP THE LINE"

ENLIST NOW — IN CANADA'S ACTIVE ARMY

Recruiting poster by A. Sherriff Scott.

battle-hardened veterans of I Canadian Corps to Lieut.-Gen. E.L.M. Burns and flew back to England.

For the Canadian soldiers who remained in England, the years of boring training exercises were nearly over. The soft spring evenings were lengthening into early summer. A sense of urgency mixed with excitement hung over every army mess. Officers and men alike existed on daily rumours. Then, early in May, tight security enveloped the entire south of England as gigantic convoys of tanks, armoured vehicles, guns, men and equipment lined the country roads in all directions. All leaves were cancelled. The huge assembly areas were cordoned off. At seaports from Harwich, northeast of London, to Falmouth, near the southwestern tip of England, fleets of warships and transports lay berthed and at anchor.

Five landing sites along the Normandy coast had been selected for "Operation Overlord." To the west the Americans would land on beaches designated as Utah and Omaha. On the east the British would storm ashore on beaches Gold and Sword, while the Canadian 3rd Infantry Division under Maj.-Gen. Rod Keller with supporting tank regiments came in between them at Juno. In all, 130,000 men were to be landed from the sea with an additional 23,000 airborne troops dropping inland ahead of the assault forces.

The Canadians embarked on June 3 at Portsmouth. One commanding officer wrote: "I could feel the tension coiled inside everyone like an electrical charge waiting to explode... troops all frantically writing letters home... a few already seasick... Outside a heavy blow and a rising sea... I remember thinking 'Thank God this isn't an airborne division....' Since there was nothing more for me to do I went to sleep."

The mighty Allied armada arrived off the Normandy coast a few hours before dawn on June 6 , 1944. As the naval and air bombardment lifted, hundreds of landing craft carrying troops and equipment plunged through five-foot waves towards the beaches. Three companies of second-rate German troops, 400 men in all, were covering Juno. Coming in against them were 2400 superbly trained men of the Canadian first wave supported by 76 amphibious tanks. Even though only 15 percent of the German coastal bunkers had been knocked out by air and naval gunfire, enemy fire turned out to be much less than expected over the last 2000 yards of the run-in. Only after landing did the fierce opposition begin. Yet the greatest losses during the run-in were caused by the static beach defences, teller mines, and the sea and tides. Once ashore four hours were needed to secure the beach before the troops could move inland. By evening the Allied toehold on the continent, although fragile, appeared secure. By day's end 574 Canadians had been wounded and 340 had died on Juno beach, far fewer than anticipated but painful nonetheless.

The Germans reacted swiftly, although not in force. Fortunately, Hitler had decided the invasion was a feint, an attempt to mask the main assault still to come across the narrow neck of water from Dover to Calais. The only Allied force along the entire front to reach its D-Day objective turned out to be the Canadian 7th Infantry Brigade. Securing the city of Caen and its nearby airfield at Carpiquet was the first goal of the British and Canadian forces. Caen provided a gateway into the flat farming country of the interior—tank country. Its airport was needed for fighter cover. According to the grand plan both were supposed to be taken on the first day. Instead, it required over a month of bitter fighting before the Germans withdrew from the rubble of what remained of Caen.

The Canadian 2nd Infantry and 4th Armoured Divisions arrived from England. Lieut.-Gen. Guy Simonds assumed command under the Army Commander, Gen. Harry Crerar. The corps and the Polish Armoured Division attached to it became known as the First Canadian Army. Slowly and surely, week after week the advance inland continued. One battle came on the heels of the next. Through rolling farmland, villages and towns, across open country, the Canadians advanced. Inefficient officers and NCOs were swiftly replaced; men fought, many were wounded, some won medals and others died—on both sides of the front. Pressed by Gen. Omar Bradley's American Army wheeling in from the southwest and by the British and Canadian armies pushing down from the north, the Germans fell back into a pocket near the town of Falaise. There on August 21 the remnants of Hitler's Seventh German Army died on the River Dives after losing 300,000 men. Having gained the initiative, the Allied forces began their pursuit to the Seine. Three days later American and French troops entered Paris.

The Canadian Army wheeled northwest as the left flank of Field Marshal Montgomery's advance into the Low Countries and Germany. No one who travelled that road into Belgium and Holland could forget the experience. In every hamlet, village and town, men, women, children and dogs turned out to welcome the clattering carrier convoys of tired and dusty soldiers, engulfing them with cries of welcome, garlands of flowers, bottles of wine and sweet kisses from the ladies. One soldier wrote: "I felt like Jack the Giant Killer... part of a whirlwind against which nothing could stand. Their happiness became so infectious that we spent our days grinning foolishly at each other or choking back our tears for having been able to help. It was like Moses leading the Israelites out of bondage—like Wellington's armies at Waterloo—and I was a part of it... and I thanked God that I was still alive to see it all happen."

In a single week the Canadian Army covered nearly twice the distance from Juno to Falaise. It crossed the River Seine, then the Somme, by-passing the Channel ports of Dieppe, Boulogne, Calais and Dunkirk to be mopped up later. The troops crossed the border into Belgium, making for the great port city of Antwerp on the River Scheldt. The fleeing Germans regrouped under Gen. von Zangen's Fifteenth Army. The days of easy motoring were over. The advance slowed, changing from a battle for river crossings to a battle for canal crossings. The Ghent, Lys and Leopold canals provided natural defensive barriers for von Zangen's troops as they withdrew in small boats across the Scheldt to the islands of Walcheren and South Beveland, where they could continue to control the sea lane approaches into Antwerp.

The Army had split. Maj.-Gen. Foulkes' 2nd Infantry Division concentrated on cleaning out the remaining resistance in the badly needed Channel ports. Meanwhile, Maj.-Gen. Dan Spry's 3rd Infantry Division (Keller, the division's previous commander, had been wounded in Normandy after an American bombing error) kept the pressure on the Germans along the Leopold Canal and in the steadily shrinking Breskens Pocket, where von Zangen's troops were withdrawing across the Scheldt. Maj.-Gen. Harry Foster's 4th Armoured Division swung wide past Antwerp and north into Holland, where its tanks and troops eventually ground to a halt during late October in the flooded polder and dike country.

PAC PA113246

Landing craft carrying Canadian troops to the ill-fated raid at Dieppe, August 19, 1942.

(Facing page)
(Above) Canadian prisoners of war are marched through the streets of Dieppe, and (below) German troops examine bodies of Canadian soldiers and their wrecked equipment

Canadian troops boarding a destroyer after
the Dieppe Raid, August 1942.

Troops who took part in the Dieppe Raid
happy to be back in England.

Some of the bitterest and most difficult fighting of the war took place in the Scheldt Estuary. To Stan Dudka, a sergeant in the 3rd Canadian Infantry Division, "D-Day and Normandy was a picnic compared to the Scheldt!" Even in defeat the German army was given its due. On November 4 a field commander's diary recorded: "Today all resistance ceased on the Lower Scheldt pocket. To 3rd Cdn. Div. and [British] 52nd Div. it wrote 'finis' to a bitter struggle. To the 4th Cdn. Armd. Div. the final clearing of the area north of the Leopold Canal was the end of something which this division had begun. From mid Sept. to mid Oct. all or part of our division was engaged along the entire length of this canal. We read of 12,812 POWs being taken... which denoted an original force of some 20,000 enemy. No one has pointed out that it has taken over 60,000 Canadian and British troops with a full armoured division to beat an already retreating and battle-weary enemy infantry desperately short on armour, ammunition, food and transport. By God the Hun knows how to put up a fight!"

In early November the last battles for the Scheldt Islands ended and for the next three months both sides settled into quasi stationary winter quarters in southern Holland along the River Maas.

Meanwhile, the Italian campaign dragged on. The troops of the British and American armies were tired. Some men in the British Eighth Army had been fighting continually since the desert campaigns in North Africa back in '41 and '42. Everyone could see the German collapse coming and no one wanted to stick his neck out or do anything foolish. This "what the hell" attitude had infected not only the American and British troops but the New Zealand, Indian and Canadian divisions serving with the Eighth Army as well. Top generals were replaced, several regimental COs were sacked and a number of battalion commanders went home for a long rest.

The city of Rimini, the eastern pivot of the Germans' Gothic Line and Apennine mountain defence, had fallen on September 22, 1944. The battle for the Gothic Line ended in early December when the city of Ravenna was taken in a brilliant encircling movement by the Princess Louise Dragoon Guards. The battle line stretched across the width of northern Italy from a few miles north of Pisa on the Mediterranean side to south of Ravenna near the Adriatic. Canadian I Corps now, under Lieut.-Gen. Foulkes, moved slowly across the Po Valley, fighting for every river; the Lamone, the Vecchio and the Naviglio Canal were crossed. The weather alternated between cold steady rain and mist to intermittent showers. The ground turned to gumbo. Four days before Christmas the troops reached the River Senio. A Christmas pause was declared.

The 1st Division war diarist reported on December 25: "Greetings were exchanged across the short no man's land but this time not with bullets. A Jerry was seen displaying a white flag then running up the bank of the Senio and in full view of our troops yelling: 'Why don't you surrender?' Although the enemy had grown tired of war too he had not lost his sense of humour.

Three days into the New Year a beautifully coordinated attack by Gen. Bert Hoffmeister's 5th Armoured Brigade on the left flank and British forces on the right pushed across the Naviglio, the Vecchio and Canale di Bonifica. This 72-hour action was described by Brig. Pat Bogert as "one of the neatest battles this Brigade has ever had." Bogert's Brigade suffered only 29 casualties. A lull developed as troops on both sides of the front settled in to winter quarters.

A Bofors 40 mm anti-aircraft gun at Point Grey, Vancouver, 1943.

PAC C121370

Frank Royal/PAC PA37479

Personnel of the Canadian Women's Army Corps taking part in a fire-fighting demonstration in London, 1943.

At CMHQ (Canadian Military Headquarters) in London, plans were being made to move the entire I Canadian Corps from Italy to join the main Allied army for the final defeat of Germany. Orders were sent. The troops were pulled out of the line and transferred to the Mediterranean port of Leghorn, where on March 7 they began embarking with their equipment and vehicles for Marseilles.

By February Allied strength in northwest Europe had reach 4 million men. Only the River Rhine lay between the Allies and final victory. The Canadian First Army, with a large number of British troops under its command, launched its offensive between the rivers Maas and Rhine. By the end of the month it had crossed into Germany to penetrate the last belt of the Siegfried Line defences in the Hochwald area south of Nijmegen. Fierce fighting developed as the Germans tried to protect the Rhine bridges, the last natural defence barrier of their homeland. By the second week of March the Allied armies were firmly established across the Rhine. As their lodgement area grew the vital north-south autobahn was cut. In the north the Wesel salient finally succumbed to the Canadians and the American Ninth Army.

With the junction of the American First and Ninth Armies near Lippstadt on April Fool's Day, 24 German Divisions were encircled in the industrial Ruhr. Three main avenues into Germany were now open. Gen. Eisenhower, the supreme Allied commander, decided to split the country in half using his American Army for the central thrust with supporting limited operations by the Americans in the south and the British and Canadians in the north. From Holland to the resort town of Baden 14 armoured divisions thrust deep into the heart of Germany.

To the northwest, beyond the River Ems, the Canadian 4th and Polish 1st Armoured Division rumbled across the flat boggy north German plain while in the south the British and American armoured divisions raced eastwards to meet the advancing Red Army. The Canadian 1st Division arrived from Marseilles by truck at an assembly point in Holland on April 7. Its last major action of the war was to be the crossing of the IJssel River and capture of the city of Apeldoorn.

The Dutch were starving. A truce was struck with the German governor of the Netherlands. Provided the Canadians held their positions until formal surrender negotiations could be concluded, convoys and air drops of food for the Dutch would be allowed to enter German-occupied territory unmolested. In exchange the Germans promised to cease all flooding and end repressive measures against the Dutch populace. For the next week truck convoys filled the roads into Holland and transport aircraft filled the skies overhead bringing food to the stricken nation. The Germans held their fire.

Fighting in Italy ended on May 2, 1945. Two days later German emissaries met Field Marshal Montgomery at Lüneburg Heath in Germany to sign the surrender document in which all German forces in northwestern Germany, Holland, Schleswig-Holstein and Denmark were to lay down their arms. During the afternoon of May 4, Capt. A.E. McCreery, Protestant chaplain of the Canadian Grenadier Guards, accompanied by Lieut. N. A. Goldie, went forward to help some German wounded. While attempting to collect them both men were killed. They were among the last Canadians to die in World War II in Europe.

In a battered hotel at Wageningen, Holland, Lieut.- Gen. Foulkes accepted the surrender of the military commander of the Western Netherlands, Col. Gen. Johannes von Blaskowitz. The 2nd Division's historical officer recorded the event: "The terms of surrender were read over by Gen. Foulkes, and Blaskowitz hardly answered a word. They looked like men in a dream, dazed, stupefied and unable to realize that for them their world was utterly finished." At Gen. Eisenhower's headquarters at 0241 hours on the morning of May 7, Col. Gen. Alfred Jodl signed the act of German surrender to become effective at midnight. The war with Germany was over. The troops started packing for home.

The Japanese war ended three months later after the Americans dropped two atomic bombs on the Japanese cities of Hiroshima and Nagasaki, ushering in the age of nuclear weaponry.

PAC PA128218

CWAC personnel with Bren guns at the Central Ordnance Depot, Toronto, 1944.

J.H. Smith/PAC PA114510

Brig. Chris Vokes (right) conferring with Maj. P.R. Bingham of the Royal Canadian Regiment near Assoro, Italy, July 1943.

Frank Royal/PAC PA130249

Gen. Bernard Montgomery standing on a "duck" to address Canadian troops at Pachino on the southern tip of Sicily, July 11, 1943, shortly after the landings that began the Italian campaign.

J.H. Smith/PAC PA114511

Personnel of the Hastings and Prince Edward Regiment in Universal Carrier advancing on Nissoria, Sicily, July 1943.

Princess Patricia's Canadian Light Infantry patrol on the main street of Agira, Sicily, July 1943.

J.H. Smith/PAC PA138269

AGIRA
670 S/M

A mortar crew firing on enemy positions north of Nissoria, July 28, 1943.

(Facing page)
(Above) Canadian troops landing at Reggio di Calabria across the Strait of Messina from Sicily, September 3, 1943, and (below) Italians welcome Canadian troops at the entrance to Catanzaro, in the toe of Italy, September 1943.

PAC PA134527

Personnel of the West Nova Scotia Regiment entering the main square of Potenza aboard Sherman tanks of the 14th Armoured (Calgary) Regiment, September 20, 1943.

A Canadian convoy makes its slow difficult way over a diversion constructed by the engineers across a narrow river near Campobasso.

Canadian artillery in action with the Eighth Army in Italy.

A.M. Stirton/PAC PA 115032

Troops of the Royal 22nd Regiment moving towards Mount Gildone, near Campobasso, October 11.

Diamond T tractor-trailers transport Sherman tanks of the First Canadian Army Tank Brigade near Manfredonia on the Adriatic coast, October 12, 1943.

D.E. Dolon/PAC PA142076

Personnel of the Carleton and York Regiment advancing under sniper fire, Campochiaro, October 23, 1943.

A.M. Stirton/PAC PA114482

A bulldozer pulling an anti-tank gun of the Royal Canadian Artillery through a stream, Colle d'Anchise, October 27, 1943.

T.F. Rowe/PAC PA142067

Left to right, Maj.-Gen. Chris Vokes, G.O.C.,
Brig. Hoffmeister and Brig. Wyman during
operations on the Moro River, Italy, December 8, 1943.

Gnr. R.J. Garcon of the 1st Anti-Tank
Regiment snipes from behind a wall during a
German counterattack on Canadian troops at
San Leonardo di Ortona on December 10,
1943. In the foreground lies a dead or
wounded German soldier, his leg encased in a
makeshift splint.

T.F. Rowe/PAC PA31064

PAC PA115191

An old woman passes a destroyed German tank near
Fossacesia, Italy, December 13, 1943.

T.F. Rowe/PAC PA116852

Canadian troops exeprienced bitter house-to-house fighting in Ortona. Here personnel of "B" Company, Edmonton Regiment, advance through the streets on December 21, 1943, and (facing page) capture several German soldiers.

T.F. Rowe/PAC PA130058

Serviceable field constructed by the Royal Canadian Engineers beside a main road in the area of Castel Frontano, Italy, February 10, 1944. The aircraft is an air observation Auster.

Dedication of the Canadian Memorial Cemetery at Ortona a Mare, April 16, 1944.

Strathy Smith/PAC PA140132

Supplies are carried in by a Jeep train of the Royal Canadian Army Service Corps on "Inferno Track" at the Cassino front, April 18, 1944.

A.M. Stirton/PAC PA139891

Camouflaged tanks of the 1st Canadian Armoured Brigade move forward to support the 8th Canadian Division during an Allied barrage.

Ken Hand/PAC PA140709

Senior British and Canadian officers observing Exercise Trousers. Left to right, in foreground, Admiral Sir Bertram Ramsay, Brig. Harry W. Foster, Gen. Sir Bernard Montgomery and Gen. Sir Miles Dempsey, at Slapton Sands, England, April 12, 1944. The exercise was a dress rehearsal for the D-Day landings.

D.I. Grant/PAC PA132473

Personnel of the Royal Winnipeg Rifles waiting in southern England to embark for the invasion of France, June 1, 1944.

D-Day preparations. This photo of part of the huge invasion fleet shows LCTs at Southampton, June 4, 1944.
F.L. Dubervill/PAC PA137130

Landing craft of Force "J" off the coast of France on D-Day, June 6, 1944. (Inset) Canadian troops eat aboard ship before the D-Day landing on the Normandy coast.

Large picture: A.O. Tate/PAC PA137007. Inset: Ken Bell/PAC PA132654

Maj.-Gen. R.F.L. Keller (third from left) and staff, 3rd
Canadian Infantry Division, landing in France on D-Day.

F.L. Dubervill/PAC PA136280

(Above) The first German prisoners captured by Canadians are guarded by military police and soldiers with fixed bayonets, June 6, and (left) troops of the Régiment de la Chaudière at a German machine-gun position at St. Aubin-sur-Mer.

F.L. Dubervill/PAC PA116532

Troops disembarking from LCI(L) of the
2nd Canadian (262nd RN) Flotilla at
Bernières-sur-Mer, June 6, 1944, and
(below) supplies being landed.

F.L. Dubervill/PAC PA132887

Four Ack-Ack gunners near the front line with one Junkers 88 to their credit, France, June 17, 1944.

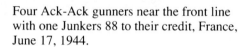

Invasion craft on their way to the French coast, Canadian troops in the foreground, June 10, 1944.

Gilbert Milne/PAC PA116339

Transport ships unloading Churchill medium tanks
Normandy.

(Facing page)
(Above) Brig. Cunningham briefs his staff before an
attack, France, June 25-27, 1944. (Below) Canadian
artillery blasting German positions, Normandy, June 28,
1944.

H.G. Aikman/PAC PA115028

Personnel of the Regina Rifles in a ruined storefront in Caen, July 10, 1944, and (facing page) a bulldozer clearing rubble. The battle for possession of the city left much of it in ruins.

Tanks and infantry crossing the Odon River on "London" Bailey bridge south of Caen, July 18.

H.G. Aikman/PAC PA116513

Ken Bell/PAC PA131392

Troops examine a German bunker on the airfield at Carpiquet, July 12.

A French veteran of the First World War greets Canadian
carriers driven by South Saskatchewan Regiment during
advance in Normandy, Fleury-sur-Orne, July 20.

Nursing sisters of No.10 Canadian General Hospital, Royal Canadian Army Medical Corps, landing at Arromanches on July 23.

Soldiers silhouetted against gun fire near Fleury-sur-Orne early in the morning of July 25.

(Left) Canadian artillery in action south of Vaucelles, July 23.

A battery of 5.5-inch guns supporting the advance of Canadian infantry south of Caen, July 25, 1944.
(Inset) Sgt. Reg Forsythe takes the sign to dig slit trenches seriously, south of Ifs, July 25.

(Large picture) Ken Bell/PAC PA116516

Ken Bell/PAC PA132729

(Right) Infantry of the 2nd Canadian Division riding into battle in Priest tanks, August 7, 1944.

Barnett/PAC PA129172

(Facing page)
(Above) Wasp flamethrowing vehicles of the Queen's
Own Rifles of Canada demonstrating their capabilities
near Vaucelles, July 29, 1944. (Below) Canadian vehicles
burning after an erroneous attack by USAAF aircraft at
Cormelles, August 8.

An ammunition truck burning during the Canadian
advance near Cintheaux, August 8.

A 25-pounder gun of the Belgian Brigade in action near
the mouth of the Orne River, August 16.

(Facing page)
(Above) A member of Les Fusilers Mont-Royal at May-
sur-Orne, August 9. (Below) A tank concentration of the
Fort Garry Horse ready to leave for noon attack from
Bretteville Le Rabet, August 14, 1944.

A convoy moves through the devastated town of Falaise, August 17, 1944.

Ken Bell/PAC PA145557

Troops of Les Fusiliers Mont-Royal carry a comrade wounded by sniper fire, Falaise, August 17.

D.I. Grant/PAC PA115567

D.I. Grant/PAC PA111565

Maj. Currie, at left with the revolver in his hand, supervises the round-up of German prisoners by a mixed force from armoured and artillery units and "B" Company of the Argyll and Sutherland Highlanders, at St. Lambert-sur-Dives, August 19.

(Facing page)
In the top photo storm boats manned by the 34th Field Company, Royal Canadian Engineers, carry the Regina Rifles Regiment's 7th Brigade across the Seine at Elbeuf, August 26, 1944. The second photo shows the begining of the construction of the floating Bailey bridge.

D.I. Grant/PAC PA136016

D.I. Grant/PAC PA137295

Staghound armoured cars of the 18th Armoured Car Regiment (12th Manitoba Dragoons) crossing the Seine on August 28.

H.G. Aikman/PAC PA144143

D.I. Grant/PAC PA141883

Some 2000 vehicles of the German 7th Army were wrecked by Allied air attacks, Rouen, August 31, 1944.

Col. D. Mingay of the Essex Scottish, Maj.-Gen. D.C. Spray and his ADC examine maps at Rouen, August 1944.

D.I. Grant/PAC PA131347

The 2nd Canadian Infantry Division enters Dieppe,
September 3, 1944.

Review of the 2nd
Canadian Infantry
Division, in northern
France, 1944.

Halifax Citadel Collection

Ken Bell/PAC PA137140

Members of the Fort Garry Horse repair the track of a
Firefly tank at Putte in the Netherlands, October 6, 1944.

Ken Bell/PAC PA130219

Tanks lined up on a muddy Dutch road at Putte, October 6.

Maj.-Gen. H.W. Foster (left) and Lt.-Gen. Guy Simonds at Eecloo, Belgium, October 10, 1944.

R.H.C. Angelo/PAC PA142097

Ken Bell/PAC PA138423

D.T. Grant/PAC PA137931

A field artillery tractor which skidded off a flooded road, Beveland Canal, October 28, 1944.

Land service mattress, a British rocket-type projectile and projector combination, examined by Capt. E.V. Burnett and Lieut. L.W. Lewis of 112 Light AA Battery of the 6th Canadian Royal Artillery, Netherlands, November 1, 1944.

(Facing page)
(Above) German prisoners are escorted out of Breskens, October 1944. (Below) A convoy of the 2nd Canadian Infantry Division on the Beveland Causeway, Krabbendijke, October 28, 1944.

Dutch children (above) with orange flags wave to
Canadian tank crews entering Bergen-op-Zoom,
October 29, 1944, and (below) children dressed in
orange paper hats and ribbons parade across the
town square of Goes after liberation of Beveland
by the 2nd Canadian Infantry Division, October 30,
1944.

(Facing page)
Sherman tanks of the Governor General's Foot
Guards and vehicles of the 4th Canadian Armoured
Division at Bergen-op-Zoom, November 6, 1944.

The 16th Company, Canadian Forestry Corps, cutting timber at Laroche, Belgium, November 6, 1944.

Troops of the Saskatchewan Light Infantry cheering Gen. Chris Vokes, in the Riccione area, Italy, November 13, 1944. Later that month he was transferred to the Netherlands to take command of the 4th Armoured Division.

M.M. Dean/PAC PA116740

C.E. Nye/PAC PA140199

The Lake Superior Regiment had to contend with flooded polders and muddy dikes in the vicinity of St. Phillipsland and Tholen Island, south of Bergen-op-Zoom, November 17, 1944.

D.I. Grant/PAC PA145657

One of the smoke generators protecting the bridge at Nijmegen from aerial attack, November 26, 1944.

Gen. Dwight Eisenhower (left) visits units of the 4th Canadian Armoured Division near 's Hertogenbosch, November 29.

H.G. Aikman/PAC PA113670

Soldiers of the Lincoln and Welland Regiment of 10th
Brigade, 4th Division, paddling canoes on the Aftwatering
Canal, January 1945, in rehearsal for their attack on
Kapelsche Veer.

Personnel of the Queen's Own Rifles of Canada on patrol near Nijmegen, January 22, 1945.

(Facing page)
(Top left) Personnel unloading shells for 240 mm guns of the 3rd Super Heavy Regiment, Royal Artillery, at Haps, February 8, 1945. (Top right) Canadians in the Kensington Regiment, British 49th Division, firing trench mortars, Zetten, Netherlands, January 20, 1945. (Below) A 240 mm gun of the 3rd Super Heavy Regiment, Royal Artillery, in action near Haps, February 8, 1944.

Amphibious vehicles bringing up food and ammunition to forward troops and bringing back wounded, Kravenburg Road, Germany, February 14, 1945.

(Facing page)
(Above) Canadian vehicles moving forward through a small forest near Sonsbeck, Germany, March 6, 1945.
(Below) German shellfire falling on units of the 4th Canadian Armoured Division between Veen and Xanten, Germany, March 7, 1945.

Personnel of the Canadian Scottish Regiment and Sherman
tanks of the 2nd Canadian Armoured Brigade entering
Emmerich, Germany, on March 30, 1945.

Personnel of Le Régiment de la Chaudière using a rubber
raft to cross the IJssel River at Zutphen, Netherlands, April
7, 1945.

A.M. Stirton/PAC PA113697

German children displaying a surrender flag, Sogel, April 10, 1945.

Infantry of the South Saskatchewan Regiment firing
through a hedge near a farmhouse, Orange Canal,
Netherlands, April 12, 1945.

(Facing page)
(Above) Buffaloes cross the IJssel River near Westervoort,
Netherlands, April 13, 1945, and (below) storm boats
being manhandled into the Ems River by engineers of the
3rd Canadian Infantry Division, Emden, Germany, April
28, 1945.

A convoy of trucks loaded with Allied foodstuffs being
moved to occupied German territory in the western
Netherlands near Wageningen, May 3, 1945.

(Facing page)
(Above) Bren gun carriers of the 1st Canadian Division on the road near Rotterdam, May 9, 1945. (Below) Children run to meet the Canadian soldiers approaching the Hague, May 9, 1945.

(Left) Collaborators and members of the Dutch SS cleaning and repairing a desecrated synagogue under the supervision of Jewish members of the 1st Canadian Division, Nijkerk, Netherlands, April 30, 1945.

(Below) Cpl. M.D. Matterson of the Provost Corps guards barracks entrance with an armed German companion, Aurich, Germany, May 5, 1945. This former German naval training establishment was later the site of the Canadian war crimes trial in which S.S. Brigadeführer Kurt Meyer was tried and convicted.

(Above) German soldiers guarding a food dump established in a forward area following the agreement between the Allies and the Germans over the distribution of food to the starving Dutch population, May 3, 1945.

(Right) Some of the huge piles of helmets and respirators taken from German POWs after the surrender.

Personnel at First Canadian Army Headquarters examining a captured German "baby" tank at Apeldoorn, Netherlands, June 12, 1945. Left to right, Maj. A.G. Sangster, LCpl. D. Boyle, Sgt. W. Farwell.

A group portrait of generals of the First Canadian Army at Hilversum, Netherlands, May 20, 1945. Left to right, seated, H.S. Maczek, E.C. Hudleston, G.G. Simonds, H.D.G. Crerar, C. Foulkes, B.M. Hoffmeister, S.B. Rawlins; standing, W.P. Gilbride, C.C. Mann, J.F.A. Lister, G. Kitching, R.H. Keefler, A.B. Matthews, E.L.M. Burns, H.W. Foster, R.W. Moncel, H.E. Rodger, H.V.D. Laing.

Karen Hermiston/PAC PA128229

(Above) Members of the first contingent of Canadian Women's Army Corps personnel to enter Germany, Hamm, June 12, 1945. Sgt. Jane Shaddock (left) and Pte. Polly Pollyblank. Pte. Martin McPherson is at rear.

(Below) Canadian troops board a train at Nijmegen to return to England and repatriation to Canada, May 31, 1945.

J.E. DeGuire/PAC PA135988

Drums of mustard gas awaiting disposal at Cornwall, Ont., January 1946.

THE KOREAN WAR AND OTHER ACTIONS

On June 26, 1950, the North Korean army crossed the 38th parallel into South Korea. U.S. forces were immediately sent into action and invited other non-communist nations to join them in this United Nations "police action." The Americans pushed the invaders back across the 38th parallel and deep into North Korea. Alarmed by the possibility of an attack, the Chinese under Mao Tse-tung joined the North Koreans. The Americans retreated.

Canada had only one brigade equipped and ready for service in the entire country and the government of the day considered it imprudent to send it to Korea. On August 7, 1950, a special brigade under World War II veteran Brig. J.M. Rockingham was created for emergency service. By September the American front had stabilized. The government decided to cut its original offering in Korea to the 2nd Battalion of the Princess Patricia's Canadian Light Infantry. Shortly after the unit arrived overseas in mid-December a Chinese attack pushed the Americans back 40 miles, but by early January '51, the Chinese drive petered out and U.S. forces began pushing towards the 38th parallel.

After a brief training period, the Canadians were placed under command of the 27th British Commonwealth Infantry Brigade and participated in the advance to Hongchon. Several enemy encounters were made during the Chinese withdrawal. By mid-April all forces were north of the 38th parallel. Shortly after U.S. Gen. Matthew B. Ridgeway replaced Gen. Douglas MacArthur, the Chinese struck again. On April 22 the South Korean army was in retreat under cover of the 27th British Commonwealth Brigade.

The Canadians and Australians held the forward positions, supported by British troops in reserve.

When the Chinese appeared the Australians were forced to retreat. Chinese troops overran a Canadian forward platoon position but the remainder of the company of PPCLIs held fast. After repeated attacks the Chinese withdrew. By their action against overwhelming odds the "Pats" saved the Kapyong Valley, losing only 10 killed and 23 wounded. For its collective courage the company was awarded a Presidential Citation.

In February 1951, a decision was made to send the rest of the Canadian 25th Brigade to Korea. The brigade was active in numerous raids and patrols. Truce talks opened in the summer of '51. The Brigade became an official part of the newly formed British Commonwealth Division. A system of replacement rotation for Canadian troops was introduced.

During October the Chinese conducted several attacks and skirmishes. Hill 355 became one of the focal points along the front and the divided responsibility of American and Commonwealth troops to defend. Twice during a tree-day period the Americans were driven from their positions, leaving the Canadians exposed and at times surrounded. Despite the severity of the Chinese attack they held on. In the months that followed during the peace talks there was little action on the front. The Chinese did make one last assault in May at the Canadian line but were firmly repulsed.

On July 27, 1953, the war ended. The Canadian Brigade was awarded first guard duty along the demarcation line. Operations of the 25th Infantry Brigade ended in November 1954. During the war 21,940 Canadians had served; 156 Commonwealth and 6 U.S. decorations had been gallantly won.

A Waco glider coming in to land during Exercise Musk-Ox, Great Bear Lake, N.W.T., April 29, 1946. The exercise was a combined land-air operation in which a Canadian Army group of 48 men, supported from the air by the RCAF, travelled across the Barren Lands from Churchill to Edmonton via Victoria Island and Fort Norman, N.W.T., to gather information on the feasibility of combined operations in northern conditions.

Other Actions

When Israel invaded Egypt in 1956, Britain and France saw an opportunity to retake control of the Suez Canal. The United Nations condemned the Anglo-Franco action and created a peacekeeping force for the Middle East. Three hundred Canadian service troops were sent to Egypt as a part of that force, followed by support troops. By January 1957, 1000 Canadian troops were in Egypt patrolling the Gaza strip. The force withdrew in June 1967. The decade of peacekeeping in Egypt cost the taxpayers $55 million.

Chaos erupted in 1960 when the Belgian Congo gained independence. Fearing one of the larger world powers might use the opportunity for a take-over, the UN arranged to send 15,000 troops to police and stabilize the country. Peace and stability returned finally when ex-postmaster Joseph Mobutu took over the country. The UN force withdrew. Over 2000 Canadians had served with the force, operating communications and providing air cargo capabilities.

War threatened between Greece and Turkey in 1964 over the island of Cyprus. Most of the island, with the exception of the Turkish minority, would have been happy to unite with Greece. Civil war erupted. To keep the conflict from spreading the UN rushed 1100 troops to the island. War was averted. A contingent of 550 Canadians serve as part of the 3000 man force.

As a member of the North Atlantic Treaty Organization since its inception, the Canadian army has maintained a volunteer force of 35,000 men and women. Their role in peace has been that of a supplementary force working with its NATO allies during combat exercises at home and abroad. During periods of strife in the Middle East Canadian forces continue to serve with the United Nations on peacekeeping duties.

If our history has taught us anything it is the futility of war. Yesterday's enemies,— Germany, Italy, Japan and, prior to 1860, the United States— are today's friends and staunchest allies. Former allies have become our enemies—Russia, Libya, Iran and the Palestinians. Sadly, it is politicians who cause the ill-conceived wars in which young men must fight and die. In the new and unforgiving terror of our nuclear age let us pray that they will be wise enough to understand the realities of global annihilation.

(Right) The treacherous Red Diamond mountain route run by the Royal Canadian Army Service Corps bringing up rations north of Pusan, Korea, January 1951.

(Below) Personnel of the Royal 22nd Regiment and Sherman tanks of Lord Strathcona's Horse meeting vehicles of No.54 Transport Company, RCASC, Korea, 1951.

P.E. Tomelin/PAC PA129108

D.L. Burleson/PAC PA133339

W.H. Olson/PAC PA115034

W.H. Olson/PAC PA114888

North Korean scenes—troops of "B" Company, 2nd
Battalion, Princess Patricia's Canadian Light Infantry, on
patrol, February 1951.

W.H. Olson/PAC PA128881

Starshells illuminating the bridgehead held by "D"
Company of the 2nd Battalion, Princess Patricia's
Canadian Light Infantry, on the west bank of the Imjin
River, Korea, June 1951.

Battery of guns of the 2nd Royal Canadian Horse Artillery
supporting troops of the 2nd Battalion, Royal Canadian
Regiment, Korea, June 21, 1951.

Men of the 25th Canadian Infantry Brigade return from
patrol on tanks, Chorwan area, Korea, June 22, 1951.

Brig. J.M. Rockingham briefs platoon and company commanders of the 1st Battalion, Princess Pats, on arrival in Korea, October 7, 1951.

(Below) Officers of the 25th Canadian Infantry Brigade examining a map, Korea, November 9, 1951. From the left, Brig. J.P.E. Bernatchez, Lieut. Vols, E.G. Brooks, J.A. Dextraze, Brig. J.M. Rockingham, Brig. A.B. Connelly.

P.E. Tomelin/PAC PA128875

P.E. Tomelin/PAC PA115809

Maj.-Gen. M.N.A.R. West investing Capt. Elizabeth
Pense, RCAMC, with the Royal Red Cross Medal, Korea,
May 30, 1952.

Sgt. Lorne Gardiner of 23 Field Squadron, Royal Canadian
Engineers, preparing an anti-tank mine before exploding it,
Korea, June 9, 1952.

During the October Crisis, 1970, curious youngsters watch soldiers and a helicopter at Quebec Provincial Police Headquarters in Montreal, October 15. This was the only time in recent history that Canadian troops were used to defend against an imagined political threat in peacetime. A stain on Canadian honour.

R.K. Malott/PAC PA144283

R.K. Malott/PAC PA144285

(Facing page)
(Above) Canadians and other members of the International Commission of Control and Supervision in South Vietnam enjoying a beer, Hoa Loi, April 8, 1973. This was the United Nations monitoring team that had the difficult task of observing and reporting on the escalating conflict between North and South Vietnam. (Below) Canadian members of the International Commission of Control and Supervision in South Vietnam, Hoa Loi, April 8, 1973.

Maj. R. Malott of the International Commission of Control examining rocket damage on police building at Thoi Hoa on June 4, 1973, with citizens' group and military representatives present.

An M-109 self-propelled howitzer.

(Left) 4.2-inch mortar.

(Below) Canadian soldiers on patrol during a NATO exercise in northern Norway.

A Leopard main battle tank of the Royal Canadian Dragoons rolls through a West German village during a NATO exercise.

A Canadian armoured personnel carrier crosses a US
Army amphibious bridge on the Main-Donau Canal during
a NATO exercise.

Canadian Forces Photo

Mass paradrop by members of the Canadian Airborne Regiment.

M-113 armoured
personnel carrier
equipped with
TOW missile
launcher.

Gunners of the
Royal Canadian
Horse Artillery fire
a C-1 105 mm
howitzer at CFB
Petawawa, Ont.

The C-9 Minimi light machine

Soldiers of the Princess Patricia's Canadian Light Infantry attack from a Grizzly wheeled armoured personnel carrier.

A TOW—optically tracked, wire guided, missile launcher.

Lynx armoured reconnaissance vehicle.

Both: Canadian Forces Photo

Canadian Forces personnel serve on the United Nations Truce Supervisory Organization on the Golan Heights between Syria and Israel. These photos show an observation post, and (inset) a Swedish and Canadian officer on duty and a Canadian Forces supply technician accepting a shipment of rations from a Polish driver at Camp Ziouani.

All: Canadian Forces Photos by WO Vic Johnson

Canadian soldiers on United Nations peacekeeping duties in Cyprus patrol the "Green Line" in Nicosia (right) and man an observation post (below).

Both: Canadian Forces Photos by WO Vic Johnson

Soldiers ford a river during a combat exercise.

A TOW missile is launched from an M-113 armoured personnel carrier.

Cougar wheeled fire-support
vehicles of the 8th Canadian
Hussars patrol during an
exercise at Camp Wainwright,
Alta.

Soldiers of the Canadian
Airborne Regiment prepare to
board a Hercules aircraft for a
mass parachute jump.

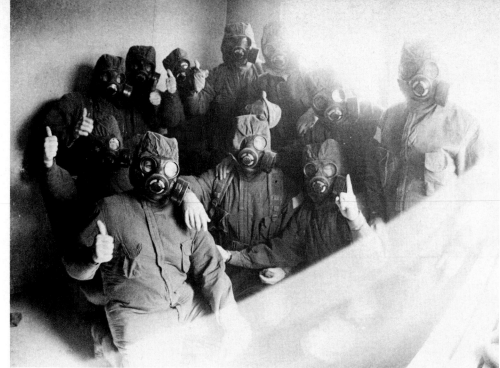

NBCW (Nuclear, Biological and Chemical Warfare) training in a tear gas hut.

Canadian Forces Photo

Training with the Carl Gustav anti-tank weapon under simulated NBCW conditions.

Canadian Forces Photo by WO Vic Johnson

SIDEARMS AND RIFLES

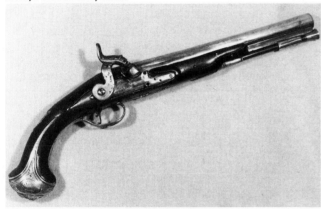

1754 Wilson flintlock pistol, said to have been used by Cornet, later Major, Thomas Merritt, in America in 1775-81 and in the War of 1812. Converted to percussion in 1827. 9-inch barrel length.

Eagle Arms cupfire revolver, 1865, said to have been a Canadian officer's sidearm in Fenian Raid, 1866. This weapon was revolutionary for its time because it was one of the first true revolvers, not a "cap and ball" but rimfire. It was popular because of its metallic, waterproof cartridges. .32 calibre.

.476 inch Enfield Mk.II revolver, 1882, used by British and Canadians 1882-1905 (NWMP used them to 1905). N.W.M.P. mark on butt. These revolvers were not strong enough for service use as the cylinders were too loose.

Webley Mk.II .455 inch revolver. The robust Webley series {Mks. I to VI) armed Canadian officers from 1887 to 1936. Early Webleys had distinctive curved grips. This is an 1894-97 Mk.II.

M 1911 Colt .45 automatic pistol. The Americans supplied the arms-hungry Commonwealth with automatic pistols in World War I. Their production reinforced our own. This is number 63 (out of 100 pistols) made by "North American Arms Company Limited, Quebec, Canada," which produced Colt automatic pistols under licence from the Americans.

Enfield No.2 Mk.I** (1943), a modification of the No.2 Mk.I (1927-38) in which the hammer spur was removed, not for a "quick draw" Commando pistol but for tank crews who needed a pistol that did not catch on internal tank fittings.

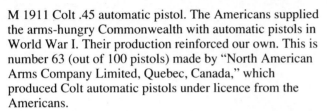

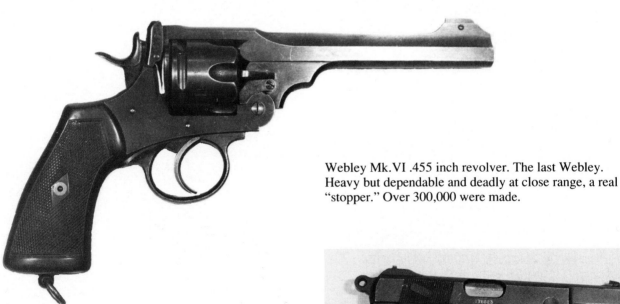

Webley Mk.VI .455 inch revolver. The last Webley. Heavy but dependable and deadly at close range, a real "stopper." Over 300,000 were made.

(Right) Browning FN 9 x 19mm Hi-Power automatic pistol. Canada was the first member of the Commonwealth to use a modern automatic pistol. The Belgian Hi-Power pistol was modified for our troops and was produced at Long Branch Small Arms Limited, Mississauge, Ont. We have used this pistol from 1944 to the present.

Brown Bess musket, "Short Land" type with 42 inch barrel, introduced 1769. .75 calibre. Brass butt, trigger guard, ramrod pipes. Lock marked "Tower G.R." (George III 1770-1820).

Pattern 1853 Enfield rifle. 39 inch barrel, .577 inch calibre. Introduced 1853. 2500 were purchased by the Canadian government in 1855. These equipped Canadian militia and regulars in repulsing the 1866 Fenian Raiders.

Snider-Enfield rifle. A Snider breech fitted to Enfield muzzle-loader. Introduced in 1866, it equipped the militia to the 1890s. 36.5 inch barrel, .577 inch calibre.

Martini-Henri rifle. Known to modern audiences as the rifle used in the movie *Zulu!*, this was adopted by the Canadians and British in 1871 and served in the Canadian Army to the early 1900s. 33 inch barrel, .577 inch calibre. It had a strong, reliable hinged falling block action.

Winchester Model 1876 carbine. A larger version of the civilian 1873 Winchester, it was used by militia and NWMP in the 1885 Rebellion. NWMP used it to 1914. 22 inch barrel, .45-70 calibre, 9-shot tubular magazine.

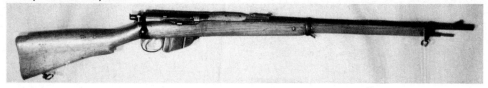

Lee-Enfield rifle Mk.I, 1896. First of the famous Lee-Enfield magazine rifles. Canada purchased 40,000 in 1896-96 and used them in South Africa. 30 inch barrel, .303 inch calibre, 10-round box magazine.

Ross Mk.III rifle (1910-16). The Ross rifle had a short but complicated history. Through 3 marks and 80 modifications, it earned the praise of target shooters and the scorn of combat troops. The Mk.III armed the 1st Canadian Division in 1915 and was a disaster. Mud and grime got into the straight-pull action, locking the bolt's locking lugs. Its weight (10 lb) and length (5 feet with bayonet) made it unsuitable for trench warfare. By 1916 Canadian's had re-armed with the dependable Lee-Enfield S.M.L.E.

Lee-Enfield S.M.L.E. short magazine rifle. This was a short version of the long Lee-Enfield. Its handy length and high rate of fire made it a great success. The S.M.L.E. is the fastest-firing bolt-action rifle in the world. 25 inch barrel, 10-round box magazine, overall length 44.5 inches, weight 8 lb 10 oz.

FN semiautomatic rifle, FN C1 (1955-85). Canada was the first NATO country to adopt the Belgian semiautomatic rifle, a highly successful firearm. 21 inch barrel, 20-round detachable box magazine, 7.62 mm calibre NATO.

APPENDIX:
CANADIAN REGIMENTS IN ORDER OF PRECEDENCE

This list shows serving Canadian infantry and armoured regiments in order of precedence:

Regular Armour Including Reserve Components
The Royal Canadian Dragoons
Lord Strathcona's Horse (Royal Canadians)
8th Canadian Hussars (Princess Louise's)
12e Régiment blindé du Canada

Militia Armour
The Governor General's Horse Guards
8th Canadian Hussars
The Elgin Regiment
The Ontario Regiment
The Queen's York Rangers (1st American Regiment)
Sherbrooke Hussars
12e Régiment blindé du Canada
1st Hussars
The Prince Edward Island Regiment
The Royal Canadian Hussars (Montreal)
The British Columbia Regiment (Duke of
    Connaught's Own)
The South Alberta Light Horse
The Saskatchewan Dragoons
The King's Own Calgary Regiment
The British Columbia Dragoons
The Fort Garry Horse
Le Régiment de Hull
The Windsor Regiment

Regular Infantry Including Reserve Components
The Royal Canadian Regiment
Princess Patricia's Canadian Light Infantry
Royal 22e Régiment
The Canadian Airborne Regiment

Militia Infantry
Governor General's Foot Guards
The Canadian Grenadier Guards
The Queen's Own Rifles of Canada
The Black Watch (Royal Highland Regiment) of
    Canada
Les Voltigeurs de Québec
The Royal Regiment of Canada
The Royal Hamilton Light Infantry (Wentworth
    Regiment)
The Princess of Wales' Own Regiment
The Hastings and Prince Edward Regiment
The Lincoln and Welland Regiment
The Royal Canadian Regiment
The Highland Fusiliers of Canada
The Grey and Simcoe Foresters
The Lorne Scots (Peel, Dufferin and Halton Regi-
    ment)
The Brockville Rifles
The Lanark and Renfrew Scottish Regiment
Stormont, Dundas and Glengarry Highlanders
Les Fusiliers du St. Laurent
Le Régiment de la Chaudière
Royal 22e Régiment
Les Fusiliers Mount-Royal
The Princess Louise Fusiliers
The Royal New Brunswick Regiment
The West Nova Scotia Regiment
The Nova Scotia Highlanders
Le Régiment de Maisonneuve
The Cameron Highlanders of Ottawa
The Royal Winnipeg Rifles
The Essex and Kent Scottish
48th Highlanders of Canada
Le Régiment du Saguenay

The Algonquin Regiment
The Argyll and Sutherland Highlanders of Canada
    (Princess Louise's)
The Lake Superior Scottish Regiment
The North Saskatchewan Regiment
The Royal Regina Rifle Regiment
The Rocky Mountain Rangers
The Loyal Edmonton Regiment (4th Battalion,
    Princess Patricia's Canadian Light Infantry)
The Queen's Own Cameron Highlanders of Canada
The Royal Westminster Regiment
The Calgary Highlanders
Les Fusiliers de Sherbrooke
The Seaforth Highlanders of Canada
The Canadian Scottish Regiment (Princess Mary's)
The Royal Montreal Regiment
The Irish Regiment of Canada
The Toronto Scottish Regiment
The Royal Newfoundland Regiment

9-pdr cannon, barrel dated 1813, carriage
dated 1840s-1860s. The British government presented 16 batteries of these
smooth-bore muzzle-loading guns to
Canada in 1856. They remained first-line
Canadian field artillery until 1874. Range
1800 yards, length 6 feet.

Royal Canadian Military Institute

SOURCES OF PAINTINGS AND PHOTOGRAPHS

Archives Nationales du Québec
Canadian Illustrated News
C.W. Jefferys Collection
Halifax Citadel Army Museum
Gravure Français au Canada
Illustrated War News
Military Museum in Montreal
National Gallery of Canada
New York Historical Society, New York City
New York Public Library
New York Public Library Picture Collection
Ontario Archives
Photo Services Branch, National Defence
    Headquarters, Ottawa.
Public Archives of Canada
Public Archives of Nova Scotia
Royal Canadian Military Institute, Toronto
Royal Ontario Museum, Toronto